THE THOROUGHBRED LIBRARY OF HORSERIDING

LEARNING TO RIDE

—AND—

OWNING A HORSE

THE THOROUGHBRED LIBRARY OF
HORSERIDING

LEARNING TO RIDE
—AND—
OWNING A HORSE

Carol Mailer & Lesley Bayley

Silver Link Publishing Ltd

First published in July 1993

British Library Cataloguing in Publication Data

A catalogue record for this book is available from the British Library

ISBN 0 947971 76 9

Silver Link Publishing Ltd
Unit 5
Home Farm Close
Church Street
Wadenhoe
Peterborough PE8 5TE
Tel/fax (08015) 4-4-0

Printed and bound in Great Britain

CONTENTS

PART 1

LEARNING TO RIDE

A good, broad selection of riders and mounts at a small, friendly riding school. In such groups will your first lessons take place, as you begin learning to ride.

INTRODUCTION

RIDING is a sport enjoyed on a regular basis by over three million people in Britain. But what is the attraction for them, and perhaps more importantly, why do *you* want to ride?

There's no doubt that riding is a good all-round exercise, testing your mental as well as physical agility. Riders soon discover that their co-ordination, muscle tone, suppleness and posture improve, and as they become more adapted to riding so they can start to employ their brain even more as they try to forge a partnership with the horse. To many people this bond with an animal is an important part of their enjoyment of the sport; athletes, golfers and footballers, for example, have only their own fitness and

Riding provides a means of enjoying and exploring the countryside, as well as forging a unique bond between rider and horse.

Horseriding continually offers new challenges. This is a more experienced rider showing how fixed cross country fences should be ridden - with a bold, positive attitude, helping the horse to do the best job.

skill to worry about, but riders can achieve little without the willing co-operation of their mount. Learning to understand, communicate with and appreciate a live animal is highly rewarding, and is no doubt why many people who are attracted to riding discover that their hobby soon becomes a way of life.

However, there's still a lot more to this riding bug! Naturally, riding provides a means of enjoying and exploring the countryside. On horseback you can get much closer to other wildlife - I've seen foxes, badgers, stoats, pheasants, hares, rabbits and more at very close range.

There are also many opportunities to socialise with other horsy folk, not just at your riding school but at horsy events such as shows, demonstrations and quiz evenings, via riding clubs, and by taking part in activities such as sponsored rides, hunting, and so on.

One exciting aspect of riding is that you can never know it all. There's always a new challenge around the corner, a different horse to ride, a new skill to master. Even the world champions in the various horsy disciplines admit that they are still learning! Having said that, you can choose to reach a particular level and stay there, or you can constantly seek to improve - the choice is yours.

Some people ride simply so that they can escape their frantic family lives for an hour. Housewives'

rides are a popular part of many riding schools' weeks, with the main emphasis being on enjoyment and relaxation.

Others start riding because they have a particular aim in mind, such as spending a week's holiday pony-trekking. The majority of young girls go through a 'pony-mad' phase, but may not be able to ride as youngsters. However, the horse bug is still smouldering and many are able to indulge their childhood passion when they start earning and are more independent. Some have to wait until their own children are grown up before they can spare the time or money to ride - but ride they do!

Whatever your reason for starting to ride, the rewards are rich - not in the monetary sense, but in terms of satisfaction, of achieving a partnership with a powerful animal, and of overcoming personal obstacles or fears, such as your first attempt at a canter or the first time you go round a cross country course.

To the ordinary onlooker riding may seem easy - after all, you just need to keep the horse between yourself and the ground! In reality it's a sport that is physically and mentally demanding. It can be elegance and harmony personified - it can also be risky. Start riding and you'll open the door to a whole new world. Just be prepared to be addicted to a tremendous sport!

Lesley Bayley

1
FINDING SOMEWHERE TO RIDE

SINCE riding is an expanding leisure industry, it would be reasonable to assume that there is a good choice of finding schools nationwide. This is, however, not necessarily so, as some parts of the country are definitely better provided for than others. Moreover, the number of schools in your area is less important than their quality. Unfortunately some areas have very few establishments and the standard of instruction and horse care is not particularly high either.

As a newcomer to riding it is important that you receive instruction which is sound and safe, and that you are mounted on a reliable horse or pony.

Traditionally, riding teachers learned their art by

One way to increase your horse knowledge is to offer to help an owner at shows and so on.

being based at a riding school, receiving instruction from an already qualified person and putting their knowledge into practice while under supervision. This still goes on, although the level of supervision and feedback a trainee instructor receives varies according to the school. However, recent years have seen the growth of college-based courses for those interested in horsy careers.

You might therefore expect that with all these training facilities available, a riding school would be staffed by qualified people, but again this is not always the case. Some people just have a few ponies, know a little bit about riding and set themselves up as places where you can learn to ride. By providing you with an example of what you should be learning and when, this book seeks to help you realise whether or not your riding school comes up to scratch.

Later the different levels of qualifications will be explained - but even if your instructor is qualified, it does not necessarily mean that he or she will be the best instructor for you. Some instructors are excellent with nervous riders, others simply do not have the patience or insight into the human condition to be able to get the best out of riders who lack confidence. In fact, some instructors can ruin a rider's confidence. This has happened to me, and it's no coincidence that many other people I know of have suffered the same fate at the hands of the same, highly qualified, instructor.

While it's as well to go to a qualified person for your initial riding instruction, you may find as you become more experienced or acquire your own horse that there are 'non-qualified' people who can in fact teach you a great deal. For instance, many top competitors give lessons although they are not formally qualified. However, they do have the necessary skills, expertise and experience.

As you will probably have realised by now, standards vary enormously, but there are some guidelines you can follow to try and find the best school for you. First, however, you need to know what's on offer in your area. Check out the Yellow Pages and the Horses and Saddlery columns of your local press, as well as the specialist equestrian press. Look for adverts on the boards of saddlery and horse feed shops, and don't forget to ask anyone you know who rides. The British Horse Society also publishes a book (*Where to Ride*) as does the Association of British Riding Schools (see later for addresses where you can obtain copies of these books).

In addition, the Scottish and Welsh trekking associations have listings of their members, many of which offer instruction as well as treks.

Arm yourself with a list of riding establishments in your area, then visit them using the accompanying checklist to decide which is the one for you.

Riding School Checklist

● *Is the riding school recognised by an official body?*

There are two major organisations in this country that inspect and approve riding schools - these are the British Horse Society and the Association of British Riding Schools. Riding school proprietors may choose to belong to one or both of these societies, or indeed neither. If a riding school does belong to these societies and is approved by them, it means that their premises have been visited and the inspectors are satisfied that a suitable standard of instruction and horse care has been reached.

However, in order to be approved the riding school has to pay a fee to these societies, and some very good riding schools are not approved because they do not wish to incur more expense with membership of the BHS and/or ABRS. On the other hand, there are some schools that are not approved because their standards do not come up to the required level.

How, therefore, do you determine which category your prospective school comes into? If you found the school via the BHS's *Where to Ride* publication or the ABRS's handbook then the school is an approved one or it would not be listed. If you heard of the school through another source, then you can check whether it is a member of the BHS or ABRS and is approved by them because it will display a wall plaque to that effect. If there is no evidence around to tell you whether the school is approved or not, work the question into a conversation with the school owner or staff.

In any case, you have to decide whether the school matches up to what you require overall, and there are many other aspects to be looked at before such a decision can be taken.

● *Local Authority Licences*

In order to operate as a riding school an establishment has to have a Local Authority Licence under the Riding Establishments Acts of 1964 and 1970, the Welfare of Animals (N.I.) Act 1972 (in

Northern Ireland) and the Riding Establishments (Inspection) Act 1968 (in the Isle of Man).

This licence is granted annually following an inspection and is designed to ensure that the horses are healthy, properly kept and suitable for the job in hand. In addition, the people supervising the rides are supposed to be 16 years or over (which is worth bearing in mind, as some places leave younger girls to carry out the 'teaching').

In order to gain their licence, riding school owners also need to hold a current insurance policy covering third party liability as well as cover for any injury sustained by the riding clients. Insurance is vital for a riding establishment as riding is a high-risk sport.

● *What level of instruction is provided?*

If you check out your school in one of the societies' handbooks, the level of instruction is usually indicated. It can vary from 'Basic instruction in riding and jumping' to 'Instruction in riding and jumping and students to all BHS exams including Fellowship'. You will see that any listed instructors will also have various initials after their names signifying the examination level they have reached. These are as follows:

PTT (Preliminary Teaching Test)
This is the first of the teaching qualifications and can be taken by people who have passed the BHS Stage II Horse Knowledge and Riding Certificate.

BHSAI (British Horse Society Assistant Instructor)
This is awarded to people who have successfully passed both the PTT and the BHS Stage III Horse Knowledge and Riding Certificate. The qualification has recently been renamed, and is now the British Horse Society Preliminary Instructor (BHSPI).

BHSII (BHS Intermediate Instructor)
This is the next level up. If you see BHSII(T) this means that the teaching part of the examination has been successfully achieved but the riding section (ie BHS Stage IV Horse Knowledge and Riding) has not yet been passed. Candidates must gain both parts to hold the full Intermediate certificate.

BHSI
This is the BHS Instructor's certificate.

FBHS (Fellow of the BHS)
The highest qualification awarded by the Society. As a beginner, an instructor holding the PTT or the full BHSAI or BHSPI will be sufficient for you. In a school where there are several levels of instruction available you will see that lessons with a BHSII are more expensive than with a BHSAI/BHSPI. You may find that you are taught by someone who is training towards their BHSPI.

Whoever teaches you, it is vital that your lessons are safe, enjoyable and that you learn from them - but more of that later.

● *What are the horses and ponies like?*

As a school has to be licensed and some choose to be approved too, their horses and ponies ought to be of a reasonable standard. However, some yards keep their animals just on the right side of the line between acceptable and non-acceptable condition. What signs should you, as a non-horsy person, look for to determine the standards of horse care?

The animals should have a good covering of flesh - animals whose ribs can be seen, whose hip bones project, who have poor, dull coats and who appear listless are not in good condition and are not suitable for riding.

The horses and ponies will be shod if they have to undertake road work, but many schools who only use the animals on the premises, ie in indoor or outdoor schools, often leave their ponies unshod or just with shoes on the front feet. However, whether shod or not, their feet should be in good repair - they should not be cracked, split or overgrown. Shoes should not be hanging off or be so loose that they clink every time the horse moves. They should also fit the feet.

Animals that are lame, which appear to limp or hop as they move, should not be working. Young horses or ponies should not be worked excessively either. Riding school life can be pretty boring for the equines; however, good schools will provide plenty of variety for their charges, for example a pony may do a beginner's lesson, a hack out, a jumping lesson and another beginner's lesson in one day instead of four beginners' lessons. Some schools actively choose to take their animals to shows regularly, giving them a change of routine. All it takes is a little thought and the animals will remain fresher.

Check out the guide to signs of health and disease overleaf for other pointers to the welfare of your prospective school's horses.

Above A useful type of horse for a riding school - not so big that adult beginners are put off. This horse will feel solid and safe enough without being too far off the ground, and is is well covered with flesh.

Below right A lighter type of horse altogether. This horse has a lot of Thoroughbred blood so the build is not as sturdy as the first horse, but it is still in good condition, with a good covering of flesh and well muscled.

Above When you are looking around a prospective school, pay attention to the state of the horse's feet. They may not all be shod, but you can see here how quickly an unshod foot breaks up. This horse has been without a shoe for just one day.

Signs of health and disease

Healthy horses and ponies take a keen interest in life and their surroundings; their eyes and coats are bright. Animals that are ill look dejected - they often stand inside their stables instead of looking out, and their coats look dull and poor. At times healthy animals will also rest inside their stables - you can tell if they are dozing as their ears are floppy and their lower lips droop. They often rest a hind-leg too.

If a horse appears to be very restless, for instance if it is always lying down and then getting up again fairly quickly, or it is trying to bite its sides, it is likely the animal is suffering from colic (a stomach upset that can be fatal).

Excess sweating and pawing the ground are other tell-tale signs. During 24 hours horses and ponies will pass around nine droppings and drink around 10 gallons of water. Each individual is slightly different but if they have not urinated or passed droppings for some time there may be a serious problem. Just like humans, sick animals go off their food and drink - uneaten feeds or hay, and water buckets that are still full, are signs that something is amiss.

If you become a horse owner you will need to know your animal's pulse, temperature and respiration rate so you can recognise when anything is out of the ordinary. The normal rates are:

Pulse: 36-42 beats per minute
Temperature: 100-101° Fahrenheit
  (37-38° Centigrade)
Respiration: 8-15 breaths per minute.

Look at the animals at your riding school. Their breathing should be easy and not distressed. After hard work, jumping for example, their respiration rate will have increased, but it should not sound excessively noisy or laboured.

If you gently pull back the lower eyelid you will see that the underlying membrane is salmon pink. Any other colouring is an indicator of problems - deep red denotes fever, and blue/red shows heart and circulatory problems.

Body-wise the animals should have a good covering of flesh. Bare patches of coat could indicate skin diseases or simply that a rug has rubbed.

Whether you are checking out a riding school or buying a horse of your own, it is important to check for signs of disease. At a riding school there will always be a mount for you, but if you have your own horse and he falls ill you'll have nothing to ride and vet's bills to pay!

● *What are the standards of horse care?*

In order to give of their best, horses and ponies need to be properly fed and watered, have decent shelter and time at liberty to relax. Your riding school may keep some or all of its animals at grass, bringing them up to stand in stalls or loose boxes to await their lessons. Other animals may be kept stabled, just going out for short periods at grass during the day when they are not needed for lessons. Whatever system is employed, there are various things you can check which will give an indication of the school's attitude to horse care.

If the horses are kept in stalls or boxes during the day and turned out at night, they should be given adequate bedding to stand on during the day. This may be straw, paper, shavings or peat - whichever is used, the stable or stall floor should have a good covering. If the animal wants to stale he will stretch out and he needs a good floor cov-

ering or he will slip. If you can see the stable floor, there is not enough bedding down. In addition, standing on bare concrete is not good for horses' legs and feet - it is cold in winter and some horses will not stale on to concrete or other hard surfaces.

It is also not good practice to leave horses and ponies standing in the sun all day long, or indeed standing exposed to wind and rain during the winter. If they are waiting to be used in the school they should have some form of shelter.

Clean fresh water should be available at all times to the horses, and you will have an indication of the feeding policy of the yard by the condition of the animals. You would expect the ponies to be reasonably clean and tidy, too - they may live out and so may get muddy, *but* before being used they should be brushed off. It is essential that any muck in places with which the tack (ie the saddle and bridle) comes into contact is removed or the pony will be rubbed sore.

One type of stabling arrangement, with the boxes built along each side of a barn-type building.

Check whether any prospective riding school is tidy - here the rugs are stored so they are easily accessible. Yards should be kept neat and tidy so that there is less risk of accident and fire. Rugs and gear heaped up in corners can also attract vermin.

Improvisation can bring dividends, for both riding school owners and prospective horse owners. Here an old road container is used for storing hay. The muck cart alongside means that the staff can muck out several stables and just make one trip to the muckheap.

● *Will I have a choice of horse/pony to ride?*

When you are learning to ride you may enjoy just riding the same horse for a few weeks. But what happens once you become more adventurous? If you are a very tall or small person, find out whether there will be a reasonable selection of animals to ride. For economic reasons one school may have more ponies than horses - that is fine if you are a small adult, but not much use if you are tall and heavily built!

Also, do not assume that all the horses in the yard are for the riding school's exclusive use. Some horses there may be privately owned.

● *Is the tack in good repair?*

Apart from needing a reliable mount for your lessons, it is important that the tack is also in good repair. Faulty, poorly-kept tack could result in an accident, so before you book any lessons have a look in the school's tack-room. It should be reasonably organised - saddles and bridles thrown in a heap on the floor should ring warning bells. Saddlery is expensive and ought to be well looked after.

You will also be able to see whether it is clean or not - but check that the leather is supple, not hard, brittle or cracked. Check the condition of the stitching on the saddle and bridle too. While it is not economical for a riding school to have absolutely top-quality gear, it should be in good repair and condition.

Above right This is an ordinary bridle made of English leather with an eggbutt snaffle bit. The cavesson noseband is fitted so that it lies two fingers' width below the horse's cheekbone and allows for two fingers to be inserted as shown.

Right A horse's tack should always fit correctly in order for him to carry out his work in comfort. You can carry out a few checks yourself. The throatlash should allow for a hand's width.

● *What facilities are there at the school?*

Many schools now have some form of riding arena; this may be a fenced off area outside, perhaps grass or an all-weather riding surface. Other schools

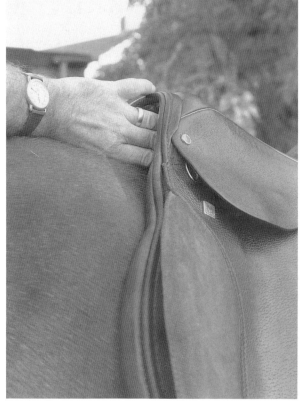

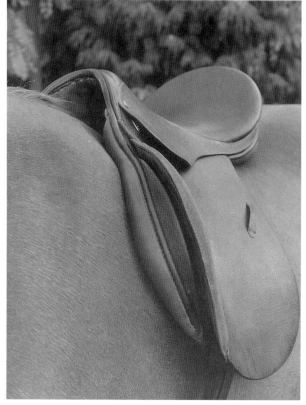

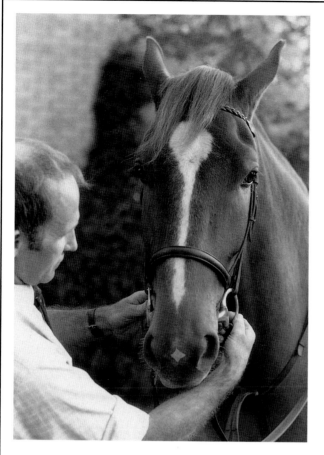

Opposite top and below left Many horses and ponies have to suffer because their riders do not fit the saddles correctly. Master Saddler Michael Longland of Alconbury Weston, Cambridgeshire, shows that there should be ample clearance at both the front and back of the saddle. You should be able to see a clear channel between the saddle and the horse's back, and these clearances should still be there when a rider is sitting in the saddle.

Opposite below right See how the saddle follows the contours of the horse's shoulder – if the saddle were to pinch the horse here, the horse's movement would be hindered and he would soon be sore.

Left A correctly fitted bit – if you can get more than one finger between the side of the horse's mouth and the bit ring when the bit is straight in the horse's mouth, it is too big. If there is not enough room for a finger on either side, it is too small.

have the luxury of an indoor school, which means that lessons can continue throughout the year, irrespective of weather and light conditions. You will usually see some jumps as well, perhaps a few stored in a field corner, or a paddock specially laid out with a course of coloured fences. A few

Below Take an opportunity to watch other people's lessons as it is another chance to increase your knowledge. Often, once you have seen what is going wrong from the ground, you can correct the fault easier when you are mounted.

cross-country fences may also be sited around the field.

Some small schools have very little in the way of facilities yet still offer excellent instruction and a good time for all - as always, you need to consider what you want to get from your riding when making your choice of school.

It is also worth bearing in mind that the number of facilities and horses has a bearing on the lesson prices, as the well-equipped school will have larger overheads.

Apart from the horsy facilities, what is there for humans? In some yards there is the loo and nothing else! Other centres promote the social aspect of riding much more with club houses, bars, lecture rooms and so on. Again, it is worth writing down what you want from your school before you visit.

● What's the atmosphere like?

If you thrive on being part of a small, friendly bunch of people, a well-chosen small school could be ideal. Or perhaps you would prefer the anonymity of a large establishment.

What were your first impressions of the riding school? Were the staff friendly and helpful? Or did they regard you as an intruder? (Make sure you don't visit the school on their day off or they may be a bit put out! Check by telephoning first). Remember that you are a prospective client and represent a regular income to the riding school, so expect to be treated courteously. If the owner cannot be bothered to spend a little time with a new client, then he or she is in the wrong business. Okay, if there's an emergency happening or a major show taking place at the school on the day you visit, you may be asked to call at another time. However, there are polite ways of saying come back another day!

● Will I be able to hire equipment?

There is little point in setting yourself up with all the necessary gear if you discover after two lessons that riding is not really for you. However, one piece of equipment is an absolute must, and that is a properly approved safety hat. Most schools will either lend or hire out hats to beginners, so check

Left It is essential to wear protective headgear when riding, and its correct fit is also of great importance. If you are buying rather than hiring, go to a reputable saddler for your gear and take advantage of his knowledge to help you in your choice. Here Michael Longland is checking the fitting of a jockey skull cap on his daughter Jenny.

Right Riding is a risk sport. For more advanced activities such as cross-country jumping you are advised to wear a back protector which again should be fitted correctly.

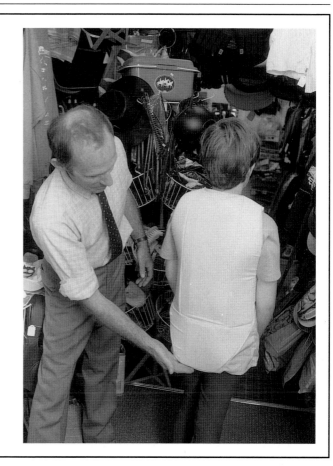

if this facility is available at yours. If any instructor says it is all right to ride bare-headed, don't patronise that school. Riding is a risk sport and sensible safety measures should be taken at all times.

Once you have made your decision, book your first lessons - if everything then goes well, you will have found a school that suits you. However, if your discover that the school does not keep to its promises - for example, if you were told you would have a lunge lesson but you found yourself in a class lesson where everyone else was much further ahead - then you will have to re-think the plan and perhaps look elsewhere.

The interim period before your first lesson will probably be one of excitement mixed with anxiety, but the next chapter will answer some of your questions and give you an idea of what to expect.

2
PREPARING FOR LESSONS

WHAT should you wear for your first few lessons? Basically, you need to be safe and comfortable. The importance of a correctly fitted, BSI-approved riding hat has already been stressed.

In addition you must pay particular attention to your footwear. Strong boots with a small heel are best. Tough shoes are okay if you really have nothing else, but they do not offer support for your ankles. Don't wear trainers or anything without a heel as your foot could easily slip right through the stirrup,

which is a potential hazard - if you fall off and your foot is trapped there is a possibility of you being dragged along!

Avoid anything with buckles, which could present a hazard. If you decide to carry on riding it is worth investing in a pair of jodhpurs or breeches, but for your first lessons wear some comfy trousers which allow you to stretch your legs without danger of seams or zips bursting open under the strain! Conversely, if your trousers are too baggy around the legs they will crease up and rub which is a nuisance, so try to find a happy medium between too tight and too loose - ski-pants made of stretchy cotton are useful.

Choose a shirt or jumper according to the weather and whether you will be riding indoors or out. Wear a top with long sleeves to save your arms from scratches should you fall off.

Riders tend to wear gloves in all weathers - they help prevent your hands from becoming sore and give you more grip in hot or wet conditions when the reins may become slippery.

For ladies or girls with long hair, it looks much neater if a hairnet is used to keep flowing locks under control.

Riding clothes are practical and have been specifically designed to keep you comfortable whilst not restricting your riding. Should you decide to carry on with this sport it is as well to buy your own gear as soon as you can.

A hat is the first consideration, followed by boots. Riding boots may be either long rubber or leather boots or short, ankle-length jodhpur boots which are usually made of leather. Adults may wear either, whereas children usually start off in jodhpur boots

Trainers are okay if you are doing odd jobs around the yard, such as cleaning out the feed room, but they are not a good idea if you are handling the horses, as they offer little protection should a horse tread on you.

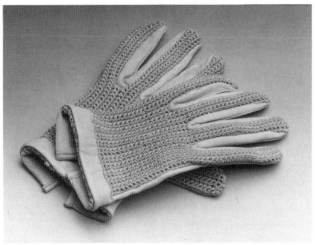

Top left Jockey skull caps are comfortable to wear - and a wise safety precaution. The addition of a silk cover makes them as attractive as velvet caps.

Top right Neatly and safely dressed for riding, wearing jodhpurs and long rubber boots.

Above Gloves protect your hands from sores and are a sensible precaution in all weathers.

Right Quilted jackets like this are great dual-purpose garments - suitable for riding and general wear.

and move on to the longer ones when they are in their teens. If you decide on long boots there is little point in investing in leather ones initially - it is usually when you are a horse owner and competing regularly that leather boots become a more viable proposition.

If you have large calves you may find that the long rubber boots are not wide enough. Some companies produce extra-wide fittings but these still may not suffice - this is why some larger adults wear jodhpur boots. Decide on the boots you are going to have before buying any jodhpurs or breeches. If only jodhpur boots will fit, you will have no choice but to buy jodhpurs - these are full length whereas breeches finish mid-calf and so require long riding boots to be worn with them.

Whilst it may be attractive to have a proper riding jacket (a hacking jacket) there is little need for one unless you intend to pursue riding with the aim of taking some examinations, hiring a horse to compete or hunt on, or indeed with the aim of having your own horse. Practically and financially it makes more sense to have one of the popular quilted-type jackets you see for sale at a saddler's shop. These have the dual purpose of being fine for riding and great for ordinary wear as well. Another possibility is a waxed cotton riding jacket. There is a huge range of styles and makes available now, so shop around for the best value. You will find all the riding clothes you need (and many more to tempt your pocket!) at a saddler's. Alternatively, if you visit one of the big county shows or large equestrian events such as Burghley Horse Trials or the Olympia Show at Christmas, there are masses of trade stands which can supply your needs.

Okay, so you are kitted out and ready for your first lesson. What can you expect to do? How can you cope with those rising feelings of excitement and nervousness? What will the horse be like? Will your instructor be sympathetic if you're worried about something? To put you in the picture a little more, let us take a look at the three important elements in your lesson before going on to the lesson content.

The rider

No matter whether you have wanted to ride for years or have decided to have a go on a whim, you will be nervous. That is only natural and your instructor will be expecting that and making allowances for it. If you have taken to riding as an adult there are additional obstacles to overcome: for instance, it can be rather damaging to an adult's dignity to be seen struggling to get on a horse, then trying to make this

animal walk, trot, turn and so on when young children are managing all this with great ease!

What you have to remember is that children are more supple and agile than adults. They often have no fear, and they are not worrying about who will cook the meals and look after the baby if they fall off over a jump! However, in a short time adults can do all of the things on horseback that children do - it just usually takes a little more perseverance from an adult.

Often it is fear of the unknown that contributes to a rider's apprehensions, but by reading this book you will know what kind of pleasures are in store for you as a rider, so you will be less anxious. An understanding of how and why horses behave and react in the way they do will help you in your dealings with them - both in the saddle and on the ground.

The instructor

As far as the instructor is concerned the safety of the rider is paramount. Each lesson must first be safe, then learning and enjoyment can follow. Instructors know that for the first few lessons a newcomer to riding will have to overcome his or her fear or nervousness, that they will not be as physically tuned-up as other riders, that they know little about the horse and his behaviour, and that they know little about riding. What the instructor has to do is:

● to inspire confidence

● to teach new skills and allow the novice to practise these until a reasonable level of competence and confidence is achieved

● to recognise that everyone learns at different rates

● to recognise that every individual's shape is not ideal for riding and so strive to achieve the best results within each person's limitations

● to be sympathetic but firm, and

● to make all this fun.

All in all it is quite a task, which is why really good instructors to whom new riders can relate immediately can be difficult to find. It is essential that you have

Above right **The essential triangle of rider, instructor and horse. Smaller groups of riders mean that more individual attention can be given to each person.**

Right Remember to ask your instructor if there is anything you are not sure about.

confidence and belief in your instructor; you must expect them to push you at times or you will never progress, *but* they should work on the premise that you are capable of doing what they ask. Your lessons should have progressed in such a way that your skills are developed and consolidated so that you are as prepared as you will ever be to make the next step.

The horse

The other vital link in this triangle is the horse, and hopefully your choice of riding school will have ensured that your mount will be safe and reliable.

For first lessons, particularly with adult riders, fairly substantial, weight-carrying cobs (a type of small horse) are often used. They are not too far off the ground and feel solid and comfortable, both of which help to inspire rider confidence. Your mount will be used to giving people their first taste of riding - remember this and let him do his job. After all, he knows far more about this game than you do! The instructor will more than likely have control of the horse so you can concentrate on what you are doing.

Meeting the horse for the first time can be a little off-putting for some adults, particularly if they have had almost no previous contact with horses. Close up, horses are pretty big, and suddenly their power and strength is very obvious! How can you control this animal? How does he think and react?

Horse psychology

Some instructors are better than others at making people aware of the horse's behaviour and mentality and how all this affects the sport they are about to try. However, a few basics in horse psychology should be mentioned so that you can handle and approach horses safely.

● Horses can see all around them because their eyes are positioned on the side of the head, but they have two blind spots: one directly in front of them and the other directly behind them. If, therefore, you approach a horse from either of these blind spots the chances are you will startle or frighten him - he may react by kicking out, for example, if you approach from behind, or by moving away if you come at him from the front.

So how do you get over this problem in handling a horse (and remember that you will soon be going up to the horse in the stable, leading him to and from your lesson and so on)? By approaching from the side you give the horse a chance to see you, and by talk-

ing to him as you approach you are giving him a clear signal that you are there. That is all it takes to avoid frightening the horse and to avoid a possible accident.

● But why should a horse kick out or bite if he is startled? Surely he has been around humans long enough to become accustomed to us?

Although horses have been domesticated for several thousand years, they have not lost their natural instincts. The horse survived to the present day because its ancestors survived attacks by fleeing if possible or fighting if they had to. Fighting involves kicking, biting and bucking to get rid of the predators, and these instincts are still strong in the horse. Scare him and he will run away. If he is unable to run, perhaps confined in a stable, and he thinks he is in danger he may kick out.

Of course not all horses lash out at the earliest opportunity: some may just jump out of the way, while others may just snort in disapproval. However, you do not know for certain how any particular horse will react at any given time so it is sensible to approach the horse properly and avoid the necessity for any reaction.

● Horses are very sensitive creatures and will soon pick up on your manner and mood. If you handle them quietly but confidently they will feel happy with you and will respond. However, if you are a 'rush-about' person who barges into the stable and makes a grab for the horse, then you are unlikely to get on very well!

As you ride more you will discover that the horses can also tell what you're feeling. If you are worried about going over a jump, the horse can sense it and may refuse the jump; he can tell whether you are positive and confident or whether you are dithering. If it is the latter he will wonder why and will react accordingly. If the rider is fretting about that ditch/roadsign or whatever other hazard is being encountered, the horse reasons that there must be something to worry about too!

The horse has been trained to respond to signals from you, and if you do not give them he is in a quandary.

● Natural instincts also come into play when a horse is being ridden. Horses are gregarious creatures and like each other's company, which is why some are awkward when it comes to leaving their friends. You are bound to come across a riding school animal who is very reluctant to move away from his companions - but turn him towards them and he is very keen to canter off to rejoin them!

There is always a reason for the way a horse behaves: it can be something rooted back in time (horses have very long memories); it could be an instinctive reaction; or the horse could be trying to tell you something (horses that are in pain, for instance from a back injury, will let their riders know by perhaps being unco-operative). Unfortunately, when the horse is trying to tell us something through his behaviour, he is relying on us having sufficient understanding of equines to be able to interpret the messages he is sending.

You may come across this if your riding school horse is asked to leave his friends - reluctance to go forward with the horse trying to nap back to his friends. Always send the horse forward from a strong leg.

By watching horses and understanding their body language you can learn a lot - they are fascinating creatures, and the more you are with them the greater your pleasure and understanding of them should be. On the next few pages we will look at some aspects of a horse's 'body language'.

Body language

You have probably read about human body posture, eye contact, and so on, and how this mirrors what the person is thinking/feeling. In the same way a horse's posture, the way he moves his ears or head, or holds his mouth provides clues to his mental and emotional state. It is an involved and fascinating subject - these are just the basics so you can recognise how your riding school horses are feeling.

Ears

Pricked forward
Sign of attentiveness or interest, such as when the horse has seen something in the distance (often long before you see anything), or an indicator that he is startled.

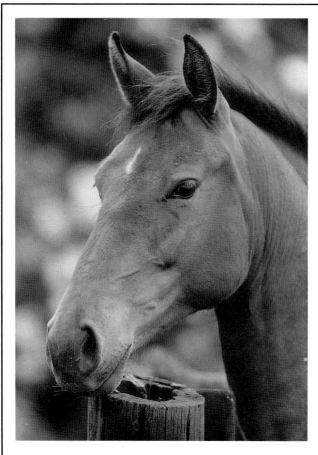

Body language: ears forward indicates that this horse's attention is attracted by something. What an honest look he has about him!

To the side
When the horse is dozing or listening to something at his side.

Back
When he is listening to something behind him, such as his rider. It can also be a sign of pain or submission.

Flat back
Anger or fear - you would be wise to keep out of the way!

Head

Nudge
A horse who gently nudges you with his head is merely seeking attention. His ears will be forward.

Thrust
If he thrusts his head at you with his ears back, it is an aggressive threat.

Jerk back and swing
If you approach a horse from directly in front of him, that is from his blind spot, he will probably jerk his head back because he is not sure what is going to happen. He will also swing his head away from any threat, such as if you suddenly raise your hand.

Head shake
Used to rid the horse of flies or dust or to show he is annoyed; perhaps he can see his food but cannot get at it.

Mouth and nose

Flared nostrils
Sign of excitement or fear.

Saggy lips
When the horse is dozing.

Tight mouth
Sign of anxiety.

Open mouth
Threat to bite - if you can see the teeth it is a strong threat.

Long nose
When a horse is going to groom a friend. Also to search the pockets of human friends!

Tail

High tail
An extremely excited horse carries his tail very high. This may be used in play - watch a high-spirited horse charging around a field - or in courtship or challenge (for example two stallions challenging each other).

Clamped tail
When the tail is securely clamped to the horse's hindquarters it could be submission, fear or unhappiness (if you go to a horse sale you will often see young animals with their tails clamped through fear).

Tail lashing
Sign of annoyance or irritation; for example, if the horse has colic he may lash his tail because of the discomfort. Some horses do so when they are being schooled and the movement is difficult for them.

Body and legs

A relaxed horse has a laid-back body outline, but if anything startles him his posture changes. Everything becomes much more alert - ears are pricked and forward, neck is arched, tail and head carriage is high and the horse may move with short jerky steps. Everything suggests that the horse might gallop off at any second.

Watch a group of horses at grass and you will see that a bossier one will often chase off other horses. His body outline will be long and low, his neck outstretched and ears flat back as he 'snakes' his head and neck at the other horses.

Presenting his rump to you is a horse's way of saying 'watch out, I might kick', whereas lifting a hind foot to kick is a reminder that his threat is to be taken seriously.

Pawing with the feet is used to investigate things and is also a sign of frustration, whereas a strike out with a foreleg means 'keep your distance'.

Calls

Neighs
Similar to our 'hello'. Each horse has his own individual voice so horses recognise each other by the sound of their neighs.

Nickers
Shorter, lower calls used at close range, for example to friends (both equine and human), or when a mare calls her foal.

Squeals
Sign of excitement, used when meeting strange horses and in courtship.

Snorts
Sign of high excitement. In the wild these are alarm signals which tell the rest of the herd that something is wrong.

Grunts and groans
Former may be used if the horse is in distress, or may be something a horse just does when making an effort, for example when jumping. You may hear horses groan when they get up or as they yawn.

3
YOUR LESSON

EACH riding school may carry out your first lesson in a slightly different way, but ideally they should follow the following lines.

Getting to know the horse
Since many people have had very little contact with horses, it is sensible if instructors spend a few minutes with you and the horse, explaining a little about the animal, for example its name, age, colour, sex, the fact that it is often used to start beginners off, and so on. This initial contact should put you at ease, especially as the instructor will probably show you how to lead the horse out of the stable to the riding area. In a couple of weeks you will probably regard such tasks as 'ordinary', but the first time you lead a horse is quite an achievement and will help boost your confidence.

Lesson type
There are various ways of starting a beginner off.

Ideally you will be 'lunged', that is the horse is controlled by the instructor by means of a long lunge line. You are mounted and the instructor gets the horse to move, stop and so on while you can concentrate on getting the feel of the animal and adopting a good riding position. The horse works in a large circle around the instructor. Lungeing requires a sensible horse who is obedient, has comfortable paces and is used to being lunged. The instructor must also have the required skills.

Some schools are unable to offer this facility, so may start you off on the lead rein; this is where the instructor walks alongside, leading you. Children are often started off in this way.

If a school expects you to control your own horse for your first lesson they are really asking too much and are not adopting the safest method of teaching a complete beginner.

Left Work on the lunge is used for all riders at all levels. You can see here the tension in this rider's hand and lower arm. Exercises will help here.

Above right Checking the stirrup length before mounting. As a rough guide, put your hand up to the stirrup bar and if the iron reaches into your armpit it will be about the right length for you.

Right Preparing to mount, with the instructor having control of the horse. The rider is almost at right angles to the horse and is holding the stirrup, ready to bring her left foot up and into the stirrup iron.

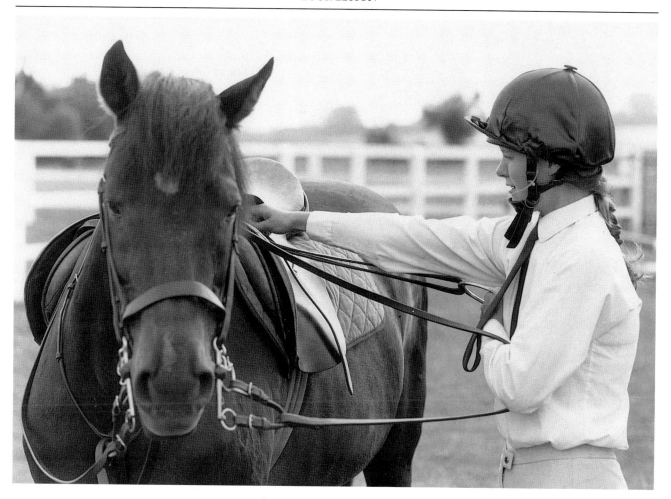

Mounting

Getting on to the horse is the first obstacle - and this is where adults can discover that they are not as fit or youthful as they thought! There are a couple of ways to mount:

From the ground

The rider mounts from the nearside (the horse's left-hand side).

- The horse stands at the halt (you would expect a riding school horse used for beginners to behave itself although, as you will discover, not all horses have such basic good manners).

- Check that the girth is tight enough (you should just be able to get your fingers in between the edge of the girth and the horse's skin).

- Make sure the stirrups are hanging down on both sides.

- Hold the reins in your left hand so that there

is no slack in them, with the spare end of the reins on the horse's offside neck (the right-hand side of his neck).

● Face the horse's rear so that your body is at right angles to that of the horse.

● Take the nearside stirrup iron with your right hand so you can hold the iron steady. Bend your left leg so that you can put your left foot into the stirrup, turning your body towards the horse as you do so.

● Taking your weight in the left stirrup iron, spring off your right leg so that you provide the impetus to push yourself upwards.

● Swing your right leg over the horse's hindquarters, being careful that you don't kick the unsuspecting animal!

● Sit down gently in the saddle, put your right foot in the right stirrup iron and check your riding position.

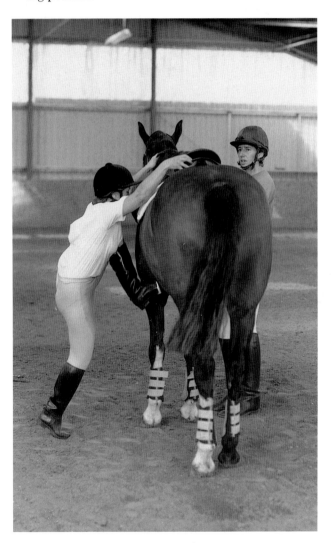

Don'ts:

● Don't grab hold of the front or back of the saddle to haul yourself up - this only results in a twisted or damaged saddle. There's also the possibility of hurting the horse's back.

● Don't get on under a low-hanging roof or you are likely to damage yourself.

● Don't forget to check the girth before mounting.

● Don't bump down heavily into the saddle - think of the poor horse! Even if you are only a lightweight it will be a shock to him to have someone crash down on his sensitive back.

● Don't be afraid to use a mounting block if you find that mounting really is difficult - you will be saving yourself hassle, doing the horse a favour and ensuring the saddle stays in good condition.

From a mounting block
Again the rider mounts from the nearside.

● The procedure is the same except that as you are at a higher level there is no need to spring from the ground. You can simply place your left foot in the stirrup, then swing your right leg over the horse.

Mounting from the offside
As you become more proficient at mounting, your instructor will probably have you getting on from the offside - this helps your suppleness and ensures that you could mount from a different side in an emergency. For instance, long-distance riders have to negotiate mountain tracks when they need to dismount and lead their horses, and there is not always the room to re-mount from the nearside.

Left A novice adult often has this problem - you can see how the rider has grabbed hold of the saddle and is trying to haul herself up. This can cause damage to the saddle and the horse's back.

Opposite If any rider really does have trouble mounting it is as well to use a mounting block. It involves just the same procedure as mounting from the ground, except that it is much easier!

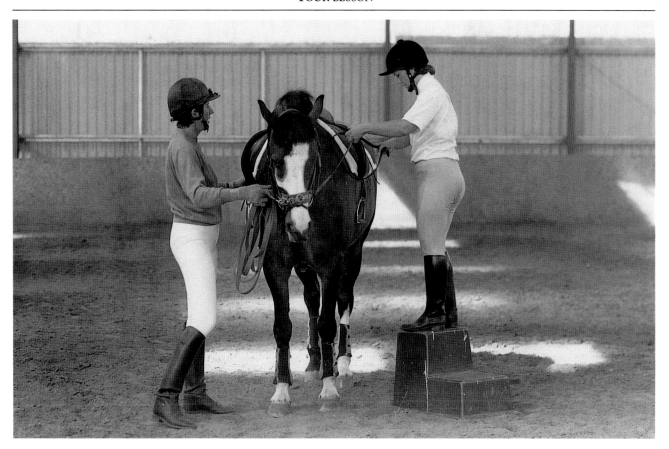

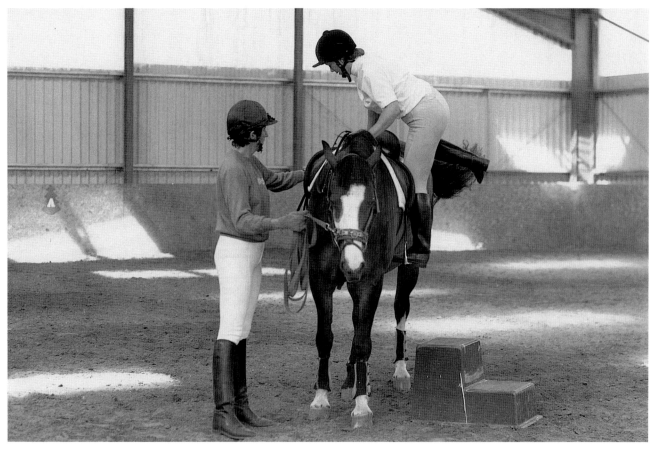

Dismounting

• Bring the horse to a halt.

• Take both feet out of the stirrups (forget what you've seen in Westerns on TV!).

• Place both reins in the left hand and keep the rein contact.

• Lean forward slightly, and as you do so swing your right leg back and over the horse's hindquarters so that you land on both feet at the same time, facing the horse's flank.

• Keep your knees bent to absorb the force of landing.

• Loosen off the horse's girth, run up the stirrups (the stirrup iron goes up the back of the stirrup leather which is then threaded through the iron). Take the reins over the horse's head and you're ready to lead off.

• It is usual to dismount to the nearside although your instructor may have you practising getting off on both sides for suppleness.

Don'ts

• Don't dismount too close to the wall of the school or you may bang into it as you dismount.

• Don't fall backwards as you land.

• Never dismount by kicking your right leg over the horse's neck and sliding down the horse's side. Imagine the awful injury that could occur if the horse brought his head up suddenly as you brought your leg over his neck.

Below Ready to dismount. It is essential to take both feet out of the stirrups.

Right With both reins in your right hand, lean forward slightly and swing your right leg well clear of the horse's hindquarters.

Below right Keep your knees bent to make for an easier landing.

The riding position

When I was learning to ride, more years ago than I care to remember, my instructor kept going on about the whole class's riding positions. Every lesson we would spend ages working on our positions, sitting up tall, moving our legs back, keeping our hands just so, etc. Looking back, it was all worthwhile, but at the time it seemed rather boring and irrelevant to a horse-mad 11-year-old.

Of course everyone should learn from their lessons, but they also ought to be enjoyable and this is where my instructor failed. How different it would have been if she had only bothered to explain *why* a good riding position was so important.

If I had been told that the riding position had been developed to make it easier for the pony to carry me it would have given all the struggling a real purpose. No one ever explained that horses and ponies are not in fact particularly well designed when it comes to carrying humans. They evolved over millions of years as grazing animals, seeing off predators by virtue of their speed and their natural instinct to flee from danger rather than stand and fight. When something landed on their backs their reaction was to get rid of it, by bucking, plunging, rearing and so on.

However, about five thousand years ago, the horse was domesticated by man and since then has served us, carrying us into battle, working for us in agriculture and, in more recent years, becoming a vital part of our leisure time.

A riderless horse can change pace, twist, turn, stop and reach good speeds from standing starts quite easily. However, as soon as rider is added, the horse is hampered by this extra burden, which is often out of balance, on his back. The horse's centre of gravity lies just behind his withers, and this is where the rider sits too, so that it is as easy as possible for the horse to carry himself and his rider.

Let's look in more detail at the riding position and its relevance to the horse

Upper body

● The rider should sit square in the deepest, central part of the saddle with his weight evenly distributed on his two seatbones (see page 42 for an exercise which will leave you in no doubt as to where your seatbones are!).

● The upper body should be tall but relaxed, with the rider's back straight yet supple, following the natural curvature of the spine. If you force your upper body into a rigidly upright position, you cannot possibly be relaxed and this will have an effect on the rest of your position and your ability to communicate effectively with the horse.

● The waist or hips must not collapse - doing so puts the whole upper body out of alignment.

Compare the rider's positions in these two pictures. The rider on the left has her legs a little too far forward - check out the imaginary straight line which you should be able to draw from the rider's shoulder through the hip and heel. The second rider has achieved this line - you can also see how much more relaxed her knee and lower leg is.

The knee should not be tucked into the saddle so that you are gripping with your knee - by doing this you are bringing your lower legs away from the horse and so cutting the communication lines. If your legs are not on the horse then you cannot give any effective aids.

Both riders would benefit from closing the fingers around the reins more - open fingers mean that the contact with the horse's mouth is intermittent.

● Relatively speaking, your head is a heavy part of your body. When riding you should be looking ahead, through the horse's ears, without tilting your head to either side or looking down. If you do tilt or drop your head then you will be affecting adversely your own balance as well as that of the horse.

● Viewed from the back, the rider should be sitting evenly and centrally so that a line drawn through the middle of your body would dissect the horse evenly.

● Whether the horse is moving straight or in a circle, the rider's hips and shoulders should always stay square with those of the horse. Your instructor can check whether your hip joints are square to the front by observing you from behind: you are fine if the centre seam of your jodhpurs or breeches is in line with the centre of the saddle.

● Think of pressing your hip joints slightly forward which will help you to keep your pelvis upright and therefore maintain a better position.

• Riders stay in position by balance, not by gripping furiously, so make sure that although your knee points to the front, it is not pushed into the saddle rolls.

Arms and hands

• The arms should hang naturally down but with the elbows tucked in to the sides so that the inside of the sleeve brushes on the jacket or top. You should be able to draw a straight line from the elbow, along the forearm, through the hand and along the rein to the horse's mouth.

• Another straight line should be able to be drawn through the rider's ear, down through the shoulder, hip and heel.

• Think of your hands as belonging to the horse - they will guide him but should never restrict. Through the reins and the bit, your hands have

Left Look up and look where you are going. If you do as this rider is doing, you will be able to direct your horse better.

Below Our model demonstrates a common fault for us - gripping with the knee and bringing up the heel.

a direct effect on a very sensitive part of the horse, his mouth, so you must always be careful and try to cultivate sympathetic hands.

● The rider's hands need to be level and a pair, with the thumbs uppermost. Try not to clench the reins or turn your wrists inwards or outwards. If you do so you are destroying the ideal line for communicating with your horse.

● You will hear your instructor talking about keeping a contact on the reins. Imagine that you are holding a live bird in each hand: you must hold firmly enough so that it cannot escape but not so strongly that you hurt it. This balance between the two will provide you with a contact.

● The shoulder and elbow joints should be flexible so that your hands can follow the movement of the horse's head.

Legs and feet

● The rider's legs should hang naturally along the horse's sides with the thighs flat against the saddle and the lower legs touching the horse's sides. How much of your lower leg and where exactly it will touch the horse will depend on the length of your leg and the horse's depth of girth.

● The rider's lower leg is important as it is this part of the body that applies pressure to the horse's side in order to ask him to walk on, and so on. The training of a horse makes use of his natural instincts - pressure on his body results in the horse moving in order to get away from the pressure. As the horse's training progresses so his reactions to his rider's signals and the signals themselves become more refined and subtle.

● The rider's toes point forward and the stirrup iron is on the ball of your foot. Think of your weight going down through your body and out through your ankles so that ankles are slightly lower than the toes. Don't force your ankles down, however, as this will only result in tension and defeat the object of achieving a springiness in the hip, knee and ankle.

The aim of this position is

● to enable the horse to carry the rider's weight easily

● to enable the rider to give effective aids to the horse, and

● to present a harmonious, elegant picture.

As a rider you are trying to achieve this riding position with the minimum of tension. You ride by balance, by staying in balance with the horse so he can do his job. Any loss of balance on your part can show in the way the horse moves, by his performance and even in his behaviour. So as you can see, there are many sensible reasons for any instructor trying to help you achieve a decent riding position.

Now you know how you should sit on a horse and why. It is okay sitting there looking workmanlike, but how do you ask or tell a horse what you want from him?

The aids

The whole system of communicating with horses and ponies is far more complex than a kick in the ribs for 'Go' and a pull on the reins for 'Stop'. Throughout the whole time that you are riding you will be having a conversation with your horse, 'talking' via the use of your legs, seat, hands and voice.

These four are known as the 'natural' aids - aids being the signals by which we communicate our wishes to the horse. Artificial aids are the whip, spurs and certain items of tack (saddlery/equipment). Novice riders do not have enough control over their legs to make the wearing of spurs a sensible alternative, but we will cover the use of the whip later. For now, let's concentrate on the natural aids. Although we will look at these one at a time, it has to be remembered that the aids are used in conjunction with one another.

Natural aids

The seat

Riders should sit with their weight distributed equally on both seatbones to give the horse the best chance of carrying their weight easily and of moving correctly. By sitting softly and in the correct position, the rider is able to use his or her seat aids to the best effect. These seat aids include the rider's weight aids as well; as you become more experienced you will learn that by subtle adjustments to your weight you can exert an influence over the horse (to indicate direction, for example). For the moment, though, as a novice rider you should just concentrate on sitting properly.

Through their seat, riders can influence:

● the impulsion of the horse (that is his energy - impulsion is contained energy which the rider directs or channels)

● the direction of the horse, and

● the outline (that is the shape the horse makes as he moves.

The legs

A horse's training and natural instinct ensure that he moves away from pressure, so to ask the horse to move on, the rider closes both legs around the animal.

The leg aids can also, however, be used individually. If you use either of your legs by the girth, the horse will move his hindleg forward on that side. Say, for instance, that the rider applies her left leg on the girth - this has the effect of bringing the left hindleg forward and slightly under the body. At the same time the horse will naturally swing his hindquarters away to the right. This can be used to move the horse sideways (laterally), which will be a useful exercise for both horse and rider at a later stage.

But what if you do not want the horse's quarters to swing away, or do not want it to move sideways? What can you do?

If, in this case, the rider were to apply her right leg, slightly behind the girth, then she would prevent the horse from swinging his quarters over. This is why, when riding around corners and through turns, the rider's legs are applied in slightly different positions.

Thus, riders can use their legs:

● to create forward movement

● to move the horse sideways (lateral movement)

● to direct the horse

● to control the horse's position, and

● to engage the hindquarters.

The seat and legs are engaging the horse's hindquarters and creating impulsion, but how is this energy directed and used by a rider?

The hands

The rider's hands are the key - they can contain and regulate the impulsion. Through the hands, the rider has direct access to a highly sensitive and vulnerable part of the horse - his mouth. Rough-handed riders can ruin horses - it is vital that all riders are aware that the slightest movement of their hand is felt as a much stronger signal in the horse's mouth.

You should therefore aim for your hands to be soft, sympathetic and still - do not use them as an aid to pull yourself into a rising trot, to keep your balance or as if you are conducting an orchestra!

The amount of contact you should have has already been covered in the riding position section. This contact should remain consistent through whatever movements or paces the horse is moving. The only

time this light, elastic contact is 'given away' is when the horse is ridden on a loose rein. At other times the contact must remain consistent or the horse will feel insecure - the horse is used to this contact (which is a line of communication) being available. If it suddenly disappears, the horse feels abandoned.

Through the hands a rider also exerts influence on the speed and balance of his mount, tells the horse in which direction he wishes to go, and controls the bend of the horse.

When a horse moves he should go forwards actively and straight; even on circles the tracks of the hind feet should follow in the tracks of the forefeet - the horse moves straight. A rider can tell whether his horse is straight when moving through circles and turns by checking how much of the horse's inside eye he can see. If just the corner of the inside eye can be seen, the horse has just enough bend. The correct amount of bend is created by a combination of the rider's leg, seat and hand aids; on a circle it is the inside hand that accepts and guides the inside bend.

In the meantime, the rider's outside hand receives and regulates the impulsion from the horse's inside hindleg which has been created by the rider's inside leg. It also assists the balance and helps prevent the horse from bending to the inside too much.

The voice

One often under-rated aid is the rider's voice - by its tone it can encourage a frightened horse, soothe a worried one, praise or reprimand. Through his training a horse learns to respond to the human voice, so do not forget to use yours!

Bear in mind though, that horses will react to voices used negatively as well as positively. By this I mean that if you are unnerved by something and you start shrieking at the top of your voice, then your mount is naturally going to be upset too!

Your voice can be used positively, for example, by counting out the trot rhythm or the number of strides along one side of the school; you will then be more relaxed, which will have beneficial effects on your riding.

The mind

The power of the mind is considerable and has an effect on how you approach your riding. Negative thinking - 'I can't get this horse to canter' - results in you being convinced that you cannot do this, that or anything else for that matter!

If you are prone to 'doing yourself down', employ the trick which many psychologists use - visualise success. Imagine yourself giving the aids correctly and the horse striking off into a canter beautifully. Keep that image in your mind when you actually try the canter transition or whatever activity has become a problem or obstacle in your mind.

Once your thinking becomes more positive this will reflect in your attitude generally - you will get on with things in a more workmanlike fashion, and you will achieve your goals.

Summary

In very basic terms the following points should be remembered about the aids:

- The aids are always used in conjunction with each other. For example, to stop your horse you sit up tall, think of letting your weight sink down through your body, close your legs around the horse and cease following the movement of your horse's head with your hands. This way your hands are not actively restraining, but they are no longer allowing forwards movement and your leg aids ensure that the horse halts squarely, is gathered together and is alert.

- Apply your seat and leg aids before you apply any hand aids.

- The inside rein provides direction and bend.

- The inside leg is applied close to the girth to create impulsion.

- The outside leg is used slightly behind the girth to control the hindquarters.

- The outside rein is used for balance, controlling bend and pace.

Artificial aids

Whips

There are two types of whips riders use - dressage or schooling whips and jumping whips.

The former are generally longer (around 30 inches) and thinner than jumping whips, and novice riders can therefore have problems with them as they can be difficult to handle. All too often an inexperienced rider will find that she is inadvertently using her whip on the horse when it is not needed. However, once control of the whip has been mastered, it is extremely useful to back up your leg aids.

For jumping a much shorter whip is used, measuring anything between about 18 and 30 inches.

Both whips should be held with the knob pushed right down to the hand so that the whip is carried lightly, lying across the rider's thigh. Check the condition of your whips regularly, since sometimes, through wear and tear, the ends come off. They should be repaired, if only with insulating tape, as otherwise they could cut the horse.

Martingales

These are designed to prevent the horse from raising his head so high that it is difficult to exert any influence over him. In an ideal world all horses would work in a good outline, but in reality some horses do evade their rider's instructions by throwing their heads in the air so that the rider has difficulty in applying the aids, for example, to steady up and balance up for a jump.

The most commonly used martingale is the running variety which consists of a neckstrap joined to a piece

A martingale neckstrap should allow a hand's width, whilst the rings of the martingale, if taken up the horse's neck towards the saddle, should reach far enough so that you can fit just the length of your hand between the rings and the horse's withers.

of leather which attaches to the girth at one end and divides into two pieces of leather, each with rings on, at the other. Through these rings pass the reins.

A correctly fitted running martingale will have no effect until the horse raises his head too high, when the martingale comes into action, exerting a down-wards pressure on the reins.

A standing martingale differs in that instead of dividing into two, it finishes in a loop which is attached to a cavesson noseband, or the cavesson part of a flash noseband. It should not be fitted to any other types of noseband.

Mounted exercises

If you start riding as an adult, you are at a slight disadvantage to child riders. Apart from the fact that children often have no fear, they are also much more supple and agile than adults. However, your instructor will probably have you performing various exercises whilst you are mounted in order to improve your suppleness, co-ordination and balance. They are also ideal for building confidence, and some of those likely to be encountered include:

● Shoulder shrugs: lift your shoulders towards your ears, relax, then repeat. This helps to loosen you up around the shoulders.

● Arm circling: individually, then together, the arms are lifted up and describe a circle. This movement should be done slowly, taking care to really stretch up. To aid co-ordina-tion, you may be asked to circle the left arm clockwise and the right arm anti-clockwise - that takes some thinking about! I've also seen instructors working riders on the lunge in walk and asking them to circle their arms in time with the rhythm of the walk, so each circle has four distinct phases.

● Ankle circling: this helps loosen up the ankle joints, which need to be flexible as they absorb a lot of movement from the rider.

● Leg swinging: the lower leg is gently swung backwards and forwards, parallel to the horse's flank and taking care not to catch the horse. A development or variation of this is to hold the leg straight out in front of you.

● Seatbones: in order to discover exactly where your seatbones are, put your reins in the outside hand and take hold of the pom-mel with your inside hand. Take both feet out of the stirrups and then lift your legs up so that your knees are well above the horse's withers. Hold this position. You should really be able to feel your seatbones now! Relax and let the legs drop again.

A rather testing variation on this is to bring the legs up and then push your knees out so that your legs are well away from the saddle.

● Touching the horse's ears or tail: this helps you to bend from your hips. You can also reach down and touch your left toe with your left hand, then your left toe with your right hand, and so on.

● Trunk twisting: both arms are held out and away from your sides, then you twist your upper body to the right and then the left, try-ing to keep your lower body in position.

● 'Round the world': an exercise performed with the horse at a halt and held by your instructor or a helper. Take your right leg over the horse's neck so that you are sitting sideways, then look to the horse's rear and take your left leg over so that you are now sit-ting and facing the horse's tail. Take the right leg over so you are sitting sideways again and then left leg over the horse's neck so you are now back where you started! Do this exercise both ways - lift the legs slowly and try not to collapse your upper body.

Your instructor will have countless variations on these exercises, and they will form a regular part of your lessons at all stages of your riding career. They are often used as part of lunge lessons to improve a rider's position.

Above right Leg swinging: a variation is this exercise, tak-ing hold of the foot, bringing it up and holding for a few seconds to stretch your leg muscles.

Right Seatbones: if you do not know where they are, this exercise will show you! Take the knees right up, being careful not to lean backwards. You can see from the bit this horse is wearing that he is not a riding school horse but needs an experienced rider.

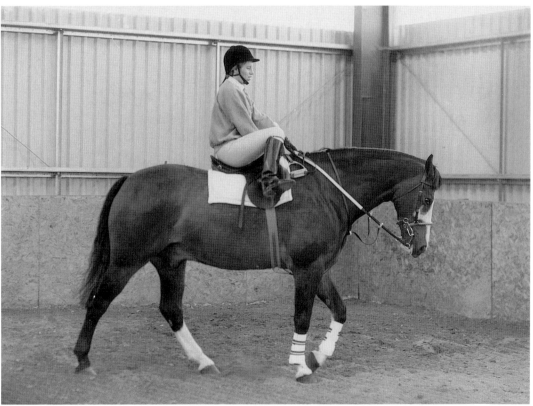

'Round the world: a favourite exercise which can be done clockwise or anticlockwise. It is great for building a beginner's confidence while at the same time increasing the rider's suppleness.

Left To start off, take both feet out of the stirrups. The horse or pony must be held by a reliable person.

Below far left Co-ordination is also improved by this exercise. As you sit sideways, one hand is on the front of the saddle and the other holds the back.

Below left Then it's right leg over the hindquarters of the pony - make sure you always lift your legs high enough so that you do not kick him.

Right Left leg over so the rider is sitting sideways again - don't worry if on your first attempts you slip off the side!

Below Then back to the front again. Now try it again, but quicker!

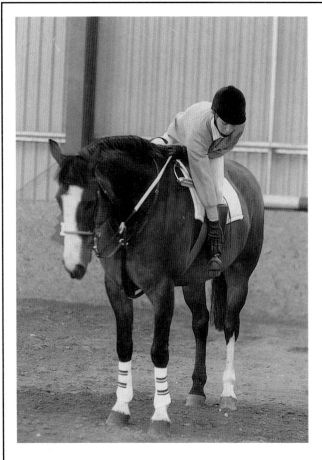

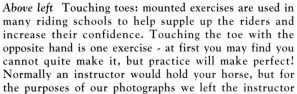

Above left Touching toes: mounted exercises are used in many riding schools to help supple up the riders and increase their confidence. Touching the toe with the opposite hand is one exercise - at first you may find you cannot quite make it, but practice will make perfect! Normally an instructor would hold your horse, but for the purposes of our photographs we left the instructor out. However, we used a very reliable horse in controlled conditions.

Above right Trunk twisting: with the arms outstretched. All these exercises are used so that riders can use various parts of their bodies independently without affecting their overall riding position.

Left If you can do this you are becoming more supple!

Above right Just to prove that adults can be as supple as children!

Expressions and commands used in riding schools

Manege/Arena The riding area, which may be indoors or outdoors (when it may just be an area marked off in a paddock, or may be purpose-built with an all-weather surface). You would expect a reasonable area to be 20 metres wide and 40 metres long - any smaller and it would be quite difficult to work in for both horse and rider.

Track The area around the edge of the manege/arena which is ridden on. In a school there is the outside track, which goes around the perimeter of the area, and the inside track which is about 5 feet in from the outside track.

Lettering You will find most schooling areas are marked out with letters and the sequence and position of these letters are universal (see the dia-gram overleaf). The letters enable your instructor to give precise commands as to where she wants certain exercises executing, and to enable you to ride movements more accurately, as you have points to aim for.

Ride This is the riders collectively who are taking part in the lesson. The **whole ride** ('Whole ride prepare to trot') means that every member of the ride is to execute the command at the same time.

Leading file The rider who is at the head of the ride and is responsible for setting a good pace which everyone else can follow easily. (**Note** that if during an exercise the leading file misinterprets an instruction and goes in the wrong direction, the rest of the ride should still follow.)

Rear file The rider who is at the rear of the ride.

Change the rein Whereby the ride changes direc-

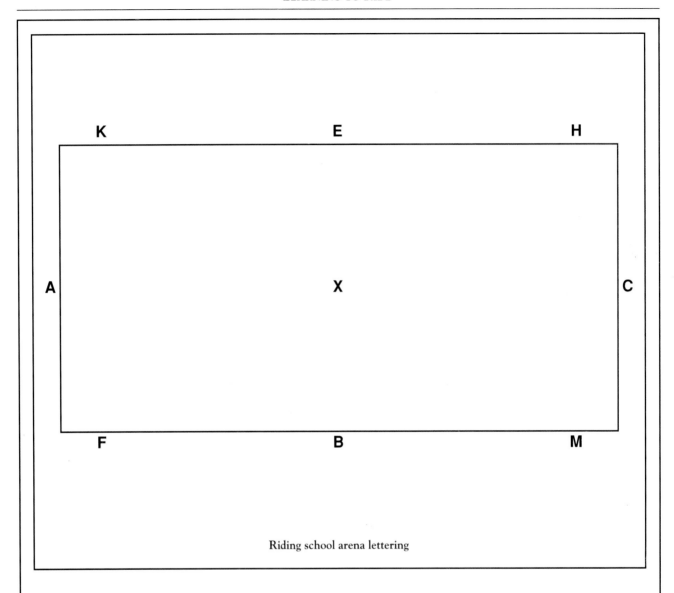

Riding school arena lettering

tion by following the command given by the instructor. For example: 'Whole ride, from A, change the rein down the centre line, tracking left at C.' Changes of rein may be made across the diagonals, along the centre line A-C, across the short side B-E, by two half 20-metre circles (A-X, X-C), and a whole host of other variations.

In succession Means that the ride should carry out the movement individually, but that the second rider should start as soon as the first rider has completed the exercise, and so on.

Distances To work in safety the riders must keep a good distance between themselves and the next horse. This distance is usually defined as a horse's length - if you can see the bottom of the tail of the horse in front, your distance is okay; if you cannot you are too close; and if you can see below the tail you are too far behind. It is up to each rider to maintain the distance required by the instructor - so close up by cutting across a corner, or give yourself more room if you are too close by going deeper into a corner.

Open order For some exercises the instructor may ask the ride to work in open order so that each person increases the distance between himself and the next horse.

Going large This means that the ride rejoins the outside track after performing a movement and continues around the outside track.

Leading file: when you are riding in a group lesson it is important to keep a safe distance between your horse and the next. If you are the first rider, you should set a pace that the rest of the ride can easily maintain.

Rules for entering and riding in a school

● Before entering the school, knock on the door and call out 'Door please'. Whoever is using the school can then reply 'Door free', so you know it is safe to enter. If you just barge through the door you are likely to frighten and upset the horses, which could result in an accident.

● Take your horse into the centre to mount up so that you are well out of the way of anyone who is riding in the arena.

● Whenever you are working in a school, whether it is as part of a ride or, later on, as individuals working in open order, you should keep a safe distance between your horse and the one in front. Do not use the back end of the horse in front to stop your own horse - some horses will kick out in this situation.

● Pass left hand to left hand

● Riders who are working in the faster pace take the outside track; slower riders use the inside track.

● Be aware of other people around you or you will cause an accident!

● If someone is having real problems with their horse, stop your own and get out of the way.

Progress list

Lessons 1-4 (individual lessons)

- Learn to mount and dismount correctly
- Learn how to adjust stirrups
- How to hold the reins
- Basics of the riding position
- Simple exercises
- Feel of walk, rising and sitting trot
- How to halt and walk on

Lessons 5-8 (group lessons)

- Consolidate all the above
- Trot - be able to rise to trot
  - learn to recognise correct diagonal
  - sitting trot should be less bouncy
- Be able to steer through turns and circles
- Introduction to canter

Lessons 9-12

- Introduction of more school movements, for example figures of eight
- Improved ability and confidence in executing turns and circles
- Be confident with trot diagonals
- Sitting trot improving
- Practise canter

This is only a rough guide, as each person's learning rate is different. The standard of instruction and the quality of the horses will also have an effect.

After the three months detailed above, riders will need their canter work consolidating and their control of the horse tested via various exercises before being allowed to hack out. Once the rider is capable in walk, trot and canter, has a reasonable seat, can apply the aids effectively and remain in balance, then he or she can move on to jumping (see chapter 5).

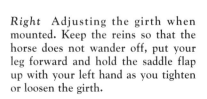

Right Adjusting the girth when mounted. Keep the reins so that the horse does not wander off, put your leg forward and hold the saddle flap up with your left hand as you tighten or loosen the girth.

Left Adjusting the stirrups when mounted. Keep your rein contact, keep your foot in the stirrup, and use your index finger to guide the buckle into the correct hole.

Useful images to help with your riding

To help you sit tall
Think of your upper body as being three building blocks consisting of:

    a) your head and shoulders
    b) your chest and midriff
    c) your pelvis and bottom

Imagine these three building blocks stacked up and neatly arranged so that all the edges meet and they make a tower. How solid that is - but imagine what happens if the top block (your head and shoulders) is slightly out of line. The whole tower now looks much less stable. So keep those three blocks neatly on top of each other and your upper body will remain tall.

To help you look ahead
Imagine a string coming out of the top of the centre of your head - rather like a puppet! The puppet master is keeping that string taut so that your head is not allowed to droop forwards.

To achieve sympathetic arms
In order to keep your arms and shoulders flexible so that they can follow the movement of the horse and not restrict him, think of your arms as being elastic bands that are attached to the reins and which have to move in conjunction with the horse.

To get a better rising trot
To avoid bumping down into the saddle for the 'sit' beat, imagine your saddle seat is made from the finest porcelain - you will then sit lighter!

4
MAKING PROGRESS

So now you know how to get on and off the horse, you know how you should be sitting, and you have an idea of the signals you should use to tell the horse what you want from him.

To get these signals or aids and their use firmly in your mind, it is sensible to put them into action, by practising starting and stopping the horse, and moving up and down through halt, walk and trot.

Here is a blow-by-blow account of the aids in action.

Moving and stopping

To move off from a halt or to move up a gear, for instance from walk to trot:

● Check your position and make any corrections with the help of your instructor. Your instructor may well help you at first by saying things like 'Prepare to move off, so gather up your reins, sit up tall, look ahead, close your legs around the horse and walk, march. . .'

● Think about your rein contact - if the reins are loopy then there are no communication lines open between your hands and the horse's mouth. Take up the reins so you have a good contact.

● Close your legs around the horse so you are applying pressure with the inside of your calf muscles.

● Be ready to follow the movement of your horse as he walks off.

To come back down, for instance from trot to walk, or from walk to halt:

● Check your position and correct as necessary.

● If you are trotting and you want to walk, take sitting trot.

● Think of letting your weight sink down through your body, down your legs and ankles.

● Stop allowing your hands to follow the movement, so that you are not actively pulling back on the reins. Use your outside rein to apply a small check (half-halt) on the rein, that is a squeeze so that the horse knows you want him to slow down.

● Immediately the horse changes pace, from for example trot to walk, make sure your hands allow for the new pace.

● Keep your legs on the horse so that the next pace is active or, for a halt, so that the horse halts squarely and attentively.

These changes of pace are known as transitions and there will be more about them later. For the moment let's think about the walk and trot, as these will play a large part in your initial lessons.

Walking

The horse's walk is a four-time pace with the sequence of footfalls being:

Off hind
   Off fore
      Near hind
         Near fore

Each time a foreleg comes to the ground the horse nods his head (the head and neck are used as the horse's balancing pole) and the rider must allow for this movement with his hands. If the hands are restrictive, the horse reacts by shortening his stride.

As the horse walks, the rider also needs a supple seat to allow for the movement of the horse's back muscles; if the rider sits very heavily and out of balance, this is reflected in the horse's way of going which loses its freedom and suppleness.

Trotting

In this pace the horse moves his legs in diagonal pairs, the off hind and near fore together, and the off fore and near hind together. Riders may either sit or rise to the trot.

Rising trot
When you are learning to rise to the trot, the fact that the pace is 'two time' helps, because you can think of 'up, down, up, down' in relation to the '1-2, 1-2' of the trot. Counting this rhythm out loud helps too.

Once you have got the hang of this, it is time to learn to ride on the 'correct diagonal'. The idea is that as the horse's outside shoulder comes back, you sit for a beat, then rise for the other diagonal. For example, if you are riding on the left rein, the diagonal pair formed by the near hind and off fore is the one to concern yourself with. As the off fore comes back, sit; you can see that the off fore is back because the top of the shoulder bulges up. Watch it and say 'now, now', then match your 'rise-sit' rhythm so that you say 'now' as you sit.

To change your rhythm, sit for an extra beat. It will take time to perfect your rising trot, but once you have got the feeling for the rhythm, start to think about your position. You will have learned to rise by thinking 'up, down'. Now think of 'forward' rather than 'up' so that the movement of your hips and body is forward, that is just brushing over the top of the pommel (the front of the saddle) instead of a distinct upwards movement.

With this horse working on the lunge you can see in action the two diagonal pairs of legs that make the trot a 'two time' pace. The nearside fore and offside hind are just coming to the ground and the horse is springing on to the other diagonal pair, the offside fore and nearside hind.

One method of improving your sitting trot is working without stirrups. This can be tiring, so you should only be asked to work for short periods in this manner, otherwise more harm than good is done.

Sitting trot

This always feels really bouncy at first, and the more you bounce the more tense you become so you find it even more difficult to sit! Your instructor should not ask you to work in sitting trot for very long periods at first, because it is tiring and uncomfortable for you and for the horse!

If you feel yourself bouncing out of the saddle, take hold of the neckstrap if one is provided, or hook two fingers under the pommel. Don't use this anchor to pull yourself down into the saddle but to give you a feeling of more security.

With the sitting trot remember to sit up tall and try to absorb the horse's movement through your lower back. It is easier said than done to relax, but if you can lose any tenseness you will find it easier to sit to the trot.

Turns and circles

Once you have mastered walking and trotting around, your lessons become more involved as you are expected to make turns across the school, ride circles and other school movements. At first your steering may be rather haphazard, but if you try to remember the aids you should be applying and look where you are going, you will soon improve.

The aids for riding turns and circles are as follows:

- inside rein for direction

- outside rein for controlling the pace and bend

- inside leg for impulsion and bend, and

- outside leg to control the hindquarters.

The object is for the horse to look in the direction in which he is moving. Although we use the term 'bend' when describing the horse as he moves

As this horse trots you can see how the hind feet are going over the track left by the fore feet - this is known as 'tracking up'. This horse has won a major showing class.

through a turn or circle this is not strictly correct; horses have rigid backbones, so cannot 'bend' as such. However, during the horse's training, he learns to contract his ribcage on the inside of the bend and expand his ribcage on the outside of the bend.

The horse's neck must not have any more bend in it than the body. Instead, the neck should be just inclined in the direction of the movement, with the horse's hindlegs following in the path of the front legs. A phrase often heard is 'tracking up', which is used to indicate that the horse is overstepping the hoof prints of the fore feet. This is considered to be good, as to achieve it the horse's hocks have to be underneath him.

However, the term can be misleading as people do not necessarily take into account the horse's conformation (shape) and how this affects his ability to 'track up'. For instance, a long-backed horse will have considerably more difficulty in overstepping his hoof prints, while a short-coupled horse may be overstepping easily, although his hindquarters may not necessarily be working actively.

When riding through circles and turns it is imperative to ride the horse away from the leg and into the hand, that is make sure you that use your inside leg and keep the contact on the outside rein so the horse does not lose his impulsion and stays in balance. Insufficient leg and your horse will fall in around the corner - it will feel to you as if he is 'motorbiking' around or leaning in. People often try to correct this by holding the horse out with their outside hand, but this does not work because to influence the horse in this instance you need a combination of leg and hand.

On circles beware of looking too far around the circle, or your riding position will be adversely affected. Look through the horse's ears and keep your shoulders and hips parallel to those of the horse. If your head and upper body are turned too much to the inside of the circle you will be out of alignment and therefore out of balance.

How to ride circles/turns

If you are riding a 20-metre circle from A (see the diagram on page 48), aim to ride a diamond shape. The points of the diamond in this example would be at A, just after K, at X and just before F, before returning to A. Horses cannot turn at right angles, so when riding 20-metre circles like this you need to think of your diamond shape; ride from point to point but round off each of the points. Then your circle should be correct. This can be adjusted to suit any size of circle.

Bear in mind that turns are always part of a circle, so the same principles can be applied to riding turns. For example, to turn from A to C, ride half a 10-metre circle from just past F on the centre line, and again from the centre line at the C end of the school. As these turns off 10-metre half-circles are quite tight, the rider must be well prepared. Look, think and plan ahead.

For instance, when turning down the centre line you need to be starting your actual turn at the preceding quarter marker. If you leave your turn too late, you will overshoot the centre line and will have to wiggle back on course. Your horse does not have a hinge in the middle - his backbone is rigid and you have an animal which is about 9 feet long to guide around a corner/turn.

It is rather like driving a car and trailer around a corner - you must allow more time and more room. With novice horses, or older, stiffer horses, even more room must be allowed, as they will be lacking in suppleness and balance.

Cantering

One of the milestones in your riding will be your first canter, and this will happen once you are secure in walk and trot, can steer easily and can apply the aids effectively.

The canter is a 'three time' pace which starts off with a hindleg, then a diagonal pair of legs and finally the fore leg. On the right rein the sequence of footfalls is:

Near hind
  Off hind and near fore
    together as the diagonal pair
      Off fore

There is then a moment of suspension before the whole sequence starts again.

The canter has a rolling feel to it which is caused by the horse's hindquarters rising as the leading fore-leg comes to the ground, then falling as the horse's head rises during the moment of suspension.

The sequence of legs given above is the correct order for the horse cantering on the right rein. However, it is up to the rider to ensure that the horse does canter 'on the correct leg'. To achieve this you need to apply your aids correctly:

• Ensure that the trot is active - if your horse is struggling to keep a trot going, there is no way that he is going to canter properly.

• Check your position and adjust as necessary.

• Ask for the canter 'strike-off' as you come out of a corner, as this is the easiest place for the horse to do so and he is therefore more likely to do as you ask.

In canter - note how the nearside hind-leg is coming right under the horse's body, providing a great springboard for the next stride.

- Your inside leg should be on the girth to encourage forward movement.

- Your outside leg is behind the girth to keep control of the hindquarters, and to encourage the horse's hindleg to come underneath and start the sequence off.

- Remember that your inside hand asks for the bend and the outside hand regulates the pace.

- As you apply your aids, resist the temptation to lean forward in your eagerness to go into the next pace. If you do go forward you will put more weight on your horse's foreleg which

makes it much more difficult for him to lift it and achieve a smooth move into the next gear.

At first your instructor may just ask you to canter down one long side of the school, the reason being that beginners do sometimes find it difficult to maintain their balance as they canter around the short end of a schooling area. This is particularly so if their mount also has a habit of cutting across corners!

Remember to sit up tall and to keep your hips and shoulders square to those of your horse. Try not to lean in around a corner or you will make it easier for the horse also to 'motorbike'.

Tenseness on your part may make the canter feel

Our models now demonstrate some problems in canter. Here the rider is leaning forward and is not sitting in the saddle as she asks for a canter transition. As the horse is not particularly well prepared for the transition, the resulting 'strike-off' into canter is not very good either.

From a poor start things get worse - you can see here that the horse's hindleg is not coming as far under as that of our show horse. This horse's head is also raised and the overall picture does not look as harmonious as the one opposite.

Left Another model demonstrates a rider fault for us - see how the rider is gripping up with the knee and the whole of the lower leg position is ruined. The horse's concern at this unusual act from the rider is shown by the swishing tail and the position of the ears.

Below left Another fault - here the arms and hands are stiff and are not following or allowing for the movement of the horse's head in canter. The rider has also positioned her legs too far forward and has also inclined her upper body forward.

very bouncy - do not be afraid to take hold of the neckstrap or pommel. With practice you will learn to absorb the movement of the canter through your loins and seat - imagine that you are riding the crests of waves and you should be able to follow the undulating movement of the canter more easily. Don't make the mistake of swinging your upper body backwards and forwards in an attempt to absorb the canter movement.

You will need to make a quick check that your horse is cantering on the correct leg - remember that it is the inside foreleg which should be leading if the horse is correct. At first you may have actually to look down to see if he is correct, but practise *feeling* if you are on the correct leg or not so that you will know without looking down and unbalancing yourself and your horse.

Transitions

Transitions are changes of pace, for example from walk to trot, with the quality of the pace before the transition determining the quality of the transition itself. At first you will just be pleased to have achieved a trot or canter, but as you become more proficient you will be able to think a little more about your riding and its effect upon the horse.

Your horse must be well balanced and have sufficient impulsion before you attempt a transition to another pace. Riders should prepare for the movement by checking their own position and keeping a good contact with the horse's mouth. It is tempting to lean forward in upward transitions and go into the pace ahead of the horse, but this should be resisted. Instead, you must be in balance to go with the horse as he takes his first step in the new pace.

Upward transitions

These are easier for the horse as he is better designed for moving faster than for slowing down. Flight is also a natural instinct for a horse, so going faster presents few problems.

When asking for a change of pace, sit well down in the saddle, have your legs firmly on the horse and

push him away from underneath you. Remember that you should always keep your legs 'on' the horse to keep a 'conversation' going with him. If you have not done this, it will be evident when you ask for a change of pace - if you have failed to keep the communication lines open by keeping your legs away from the horse's sides, the aid for the transition will shock the poor animal. One minute there are no instructions from your legs, the next the horse is being told to trot or canter on. In such cases the horse often reacts by going hollow (his outline is no longer rounded) and shortening his steps.

Going into the next pace ahead of the horse is a common problem. When riders anticipate a transition, tip forward and drop the contact, there is nothing for the horse to go forwards into, and he has no choice but to fall into the transition and the next pace rather than going forwards, in balance, into the trot or canter.

To achieve a good transition the horse must be balanced, active and responsive to the rider's leg. If the horse is failing to respond to the leg, the transition will be sluggish. If the horse is not answering to your leg then any attempt at a transition be poor, so it is vital to establish a good, active pace before trying to move up a gear.

Preparation is vital for a successful transition or the horse will be on his forehand. It is important that the rider maintains a good sympathetic contact throughout the transition. However, letting the reins go is another common fault.

Transitions from trot to canter will magnify faults. Some riders are too restrictive with their hands so their mounts raise their heads and necks and are generally resistant.

Downwards transitions

These are more difficult for the horse as he tends to fall on to his forehand in the transition. To counteract this the use of 'half halts' is advisable. A half halt is a signal from the rider to the horse which has the effect of saying 'Pay attention, we're about to do something'.

To half halt, the rider sits in the saddle with both legs closed firmly around the horse. Then the rider checks (that is squeezes firmly) on the outside rein whilst still maintaining the bend in the direction of the movement with the inside rein. It is vital that when using the half halt the rider uses sufficient leg to keep the hocks underneath the horse. The balance of the communication here, between hand and leg, is essential to the success of the half halt and the following transition.

In the early stages of both a rider's and a horse's training, all transitions should be progressive - they should come down from trot to walk and then halt. Acute transitions are those involving a move from one pace to another without an intervening pace, as for example going straight from halt to trot.

A horse's conformation or design is not particularly well suited to downward transitions. Nature intends a horse to take the strain of halting on his hind legs, for these have the hock joint which bends. Watch a horse skidding up to a gate in a field and you will see how his hindquarters lower and his hocks bend to cushion the effect of stopping. However, with a rider on top, the weight is pushed forward, so it is the horse's forelegs that have to take more of the strain. This is why the most common problem with downwards transitions is the horse falling on to his forehand.

Riders who are 'out of sync' with their horses only add to his difficulties in performing any transition. Take, for example, the rider who leans back and pulls as she tries to bring her horse down a gear. The result will not only look very untidy and uncouth, but will also upset the horse, so the quality of the pace following the transition will be affected adversely.

Riding school movements

A creative riding instructor will use a whole host of school movements to keep your lessons interesting while still giving you the chance to practise skills, improve your feel for the horse's movement and help your co-ordination.

School movements are intended to help your suppleness as well as that of the horse. They also show how much control you have over the animal and how clear or otherwise your aids are.

One of the most difficult things in riding is to keep the horse straight - wobbly lines are common problems, as are odd-shaped circles, horses and riders falling in around corners (also known as 'motor-biking'), inaccuracies when executing movements, such as leaving the track too early or turning too late, to name but a few.

But why will your instructor insist on getting school movements right? For a start, it is a good way of instilling discipline into both horse and rider. As far as the rider is concerned, self-discipline will be needed if you are to progress and will certainly be needed in abundance if you ever wish to own a horse. From the horse's point of view, it is vital for his muscular development that exercises are carried out correctly, whilst the obedience required makes for a more pleasant riding animal.

Some of the common movements are examined later, but there are some general rules that need to be observed at all times:

● Think about what you are doing and prepare in advance.

● Look ahead - if you do not know where you are going, the movement is doomed to failure.

● Ensure you keep as good a position as possible - make checks every now and then to keep you on your toes.

● Ride with confidence and a positive attitude. If it helps, imagine yourself as a top rider!

● Read about the theory behind schoolwork and this should also help your practical application.

● Beware of trying too hard and creating tension in your body.

● Ensure that your instructions to the horse are crystal clear.

The arena

Most riders will use a 20 m by 40 m school, so if you are executing a 20-metre circle at A you are effectively using half the school.

The corners tend to be the most underused area in a school as many riders cut across them. If the horse you are riding is old and stiff, you have an excuse for riding a shallower corner, but otherwise you should aim to go deep into the corner, using your inside leg to push the horse over.

Something that will help you and your horse is to ride a circle in each corner. Ensure you start off in walk until you have the co-ordination of your aids under control, then you can try in trot. Remember to ride from your inside leg to outside hand - your inside leg is encouraging the horse over, and the outside rein is held with a steady contact so that the horse does not fall out through his shoulder.

Think of riding your horse in a channel made by your hands and legs - the horse moves within this channel wherever you ask him to go.

Circles

These are generally ridden as 20, 15 or 10 metre circles. You can see from the 20-metre circle diagram where three circles may be ridden in a 20 m by 40 m arena. Note where each circle touches the track and where its other points of contact are. Where the circles touch the track, this is for one stride only.

Riding a true circle is a difficult exercise, and any unevenness or stiffness on the part of the horse or rider soon shows up. The horse should be bent throughout the length of his body (although the horse's spine is fairly rigid so it is his side muscles that stretch and contract to allow bend). The horse's hind

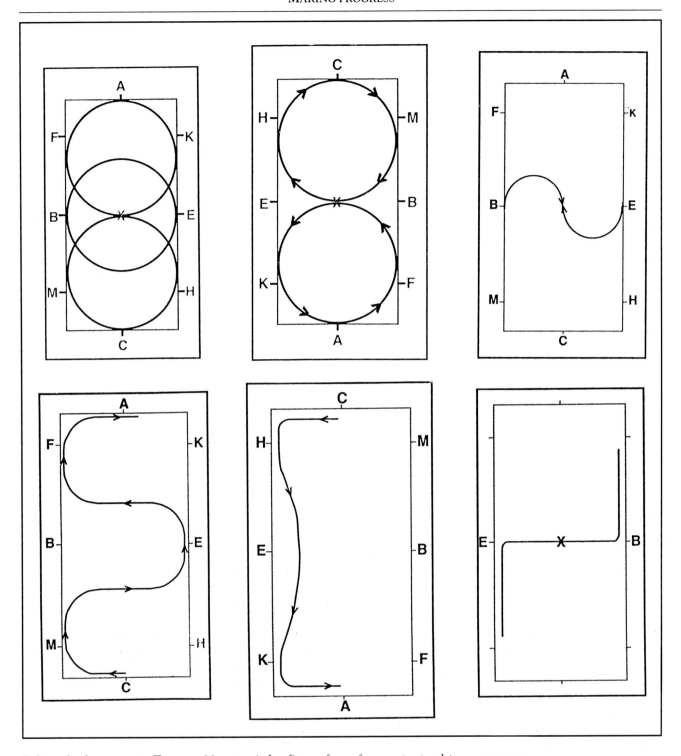

Riding school movements. Top row: 20-metre circles, figure of eight, and half-circles; bottom row: three-loop serpentine, shallow loop, and changing rein across the school.

feet should follow in the track of his front feet and your shoulders should match those of the horse. If you can just see the corner of the horse's inside eye you have sufficient bend. Remember to keep your outside leg just behind the girth to prevent the horse from swinging his quarters out.

With 20-metre circles you have various exercises, such as three 20-metre circles ridden consecutively at A, B and C; or a figure of eight using two 20-metre circles. With this exercise you need to ride a short straight line over X so you can change the bend and the rein. You may ride half a 20-metre circle from A to X, then another half-20-metre circle from X to C. Again, it is the change across X that presents most problems. You need to plan well in advance so that you swop your aids over and change the bend in time.

Smaller circles such as 15 and 10 metre ones present even more problems and require a fairly supple animal. If you ride a 15-metre circle from E, the circle will pass over the three-quarter line for one stride (the three-quarter line is an imaginary line which, in this case, would pass halfway between X and B and run parallel to the F/B/M long side). A 15-metre circle ridden at the A or C end of the school would be 2.5 metres in from each long side of the arena.

Ten-metre circles, ridden from the long sides, pass over the centre line (the imaginary line which runs from A to C) for one stride.

The principles you apply to riding 20-metre circles come into play for smaller circles, but as everything happens much quicker it is sensible to start working in 15 and then 10-metre circles in walk so you can accustom yourself to producing the correct shape before moving up a gear. When riding circles of 10 metres in trot you should take sitting trot.

Half-10-metre circles, for example from B to X, or X to E, can also be used to change the rein or as an exercise in themselves. The difficulty often lies in keeping the correct flexion: planning and looking ahead is vital. For instance, come off the track four steps after B and follow a nicely shaped arc, remembering to look where you are going. You will come on to the centre line four steps before X and leave the centre line to start your other half circle four steps after X, ie there is one straight stride through X. At X you need to change the flexion in preparation for the second half-circle and you will rejoin the outside track four steps before E.

Serpentines

These may consist of three or four loops which all need to be of equal proportion. Serpentines using more loops can be ridden but these would tend to be used by the more advanced riders. The art lies in producing half-circles at the end of each loop followed in very quick succession by straight lines, so you need to know exactly where you are going in order to give yourself the chance to concentrate on co-ordinating your aids. The use of half halts before each half-circle is a great help and you need to start off by making full use of the corner before you begin your serpentine.

For example, if you are riding a three-loop serpentine beginning at C you must first establish an active sitting trot. Make good use of the corner and execute a half-circle, half halting before you ride straight across the centre line, aiming for a point approximately half way between H and E. Half halt and change your flexion so that three-quarters of the way

across you can start to ride another half-circle (rejoining the track four steps before E and leaving it four steps after E). Remember to half halt before you ride straight and repeat the moves so that you complete another loop to finish at A. If you execute this exercise in rising trot, remember to change the rein each time you cross the centre line.

Loops

These may be ridden off the long side or along the centre line. They are useful for suppling the horse and for teaching the rider about changing the bend.

A loop off the long side may be ridden so that the apex of the loop (at either B or E) is 3 or 5 metres in from the track. If you are riding a loop on the left rein off the H/E/K long side your horse will have left bend as you come around the C/H corner and start the loop, four steps after H. From that point until you complete the loop four steps before rejoining the track at K, the horse will have right bend. When you have completed the loop, ie four steps before K, you need to change the bend back to left bend. The same principles apply if you ride shallow 3-metre loops along the centre line.

Changes of rein

There are numerous ways of doing this but the most common ones used for beginner riders are diagonal changes and changing across the school, for example from B to E or from A to C, and vice versa.

For the diagonal change of rein, for example on the right rein from M through X to K, the problem that usually occurs is that the rider does not prepare well enough for the turn and turns late, then has to wiggle her way back on course. The horse often loses impulsion through turns, so you must be ready with your inside leg to maintain the impulsion and rhythm throughout the exercise.

Give yourself enough room at the far end of the diagonal to make a decent turn around the circle - aim to meet the track before the actual marker so you do not cut across the corner.

For changes from B to E and vice versa, think of making a quarter-circle from B or E four steps before the marker. Look straight across to your other marker and start to change the flexion as you go over X, making another quarter-circle four steps before you reach the marker so you make a smooth turn on to the track.

Riding out

When you have learned the basics of riding, and can walk, trot, canter and stop easily, you are bound to

A group of riders enjoying a hack out from their riding school.

want to broaden your horizons. The idea of riding out (or 'hacking') in the countryside is appealing. However, cantering across vast open spaces such as fields, commons or moorland is totally different from riding within the confines of a schooling arena, whether it is inside or out. Your horse may suddenly find some extra spark, and an animal that used to be quite easy to slow down or stop may become much more difficult. When you're riding in company, a canter can develop into a race quite easily.

In order to prepare you for riding out, many instructors will build your skill and confidence by undertaking small exercises outdoors at your riding school. For instance, you may be asked to leave the ride, make your way to a certain point in the field, then trot back to the rest of the ride. Perhaps you will go off in pairs for a trot, maybe you will canter back to the ride or warm your horses up individually in the paddock.

Such experiences will give you the chance to discover how horses react on their own, how they sometimes take charge or become more difficult to handle. Once you can cope with these sort of lessons confidently, you will also be able to handle riding out.

For safety purposes your riding school should ideally provide one experienced escort for every four or five riders. If it is at all possible, it is safest to have an experienced rider at the rear of the ride as well as at the front. Your leading escort should give plenty of notice that she is about to trot on, walk, canter, etc, and the pace of the ride should be adjusted according to the ability of the least competent rider.

When riding outside it is just as important to maintain sensible distances between the horses as inside. Remember, too, to be aware of everyone else - a rider in front could fall off as quickly as you can blink, so be alert!

Your first experience of hacking can have an effect on how you regard riding out for ever more, so do all you can to make it enjoyable. If you find that your horse is a little too lively for you, ask the instructor if you can swop. A friend of mine was over-horsed on her first ride out, was run away with and suffered a nasty fall. It was the first dent in her confidence and unfortunately similar experiences at the same riding school meant that she gave up riding soon after!

However, there are other difficulties apart from remaining in control when you ride outdoors. Tackling hills or uneven terrain, negotiating roads and opening gates can all pose problems. Remember that even the most experienced horse can be suddenly spooked by something on the road.

It is therefore vital when riding on the road to ride properly at all times. Never daydream along. Take note of the signals your instructor uses as she leads the ride along - it is a good way to learn the rider's highway code. If your ride has to cross over another road, the escorts should make sure that the whole ride moves over together. They should not allow the ride to split so that some are on one side and the others are opposite; such a situation may upset the horses and could result in a horse taking charge and rushing off to rejoin his friends, the results of which could be disastrous.

Riding up and down hills

To negotiate steep hills make sure your weight is well forward so that the horse's back is free. Keep your weight over your knees and hold on to the mane if necessary to balance yourself. Do not use the reins as a balancing aid - your horse needs the freedom of his head and neck to balance himself.

Always take the direct route down a steep hill - do not zigzag your way down as the horse could easily lose his footing and slip. Sit tall in your saddle, neither leaning backwards nor forwards, but taking your weight down through your legs and heels. Again, your horse must have freedom to balance himself.

Gates

Your instructor/escort will no doubt open the gate for the ride, but you may get the chance to try it for yourself. If so, try to position your horse parallel to the gate with his head facing the latch. Take

the reins and whip in one hand and undo the latch with the hand nearest the gate. Use your leg nearest the gate to ask your horse to move away from it (the horse will be turning on the forehand).

Open the gate sufficiently so that you can pass through - some horses do become upset and try to rush through. Give yourself enough room or you could be knocked off and injured.

Once through, position your horse parallel to the gate again so you can pull it to and fasten the latch. Always be aware of the position of your horse's head - it is quite easy for a horse to catch his bridle on a gate latch.

Strong horses

You will find that riding school horses and ponies will know their hacks and will know where to canter, where to slow down, and so on. If you find that your horse is becoming rather strong, 'bridging' the reins may help. This will ensure that the horse does not pull the reins from you, unbalancing you in the process. If you have a relatively stable position in the saddle and find yourself moving faster than you would like, try this method of slowing a horse: anchor one hand in the horse's mane and with the other rein give short sharp tugs. If you just pull constantly against a horse he will only pull harder against you.

Whatever you do, do not scream if you find yourself going much faster than you have ever been before. You will probably only succeed in scaring the horse, and making him go faster to escape the wailing monster! Make sure you sit up - often novices lean forwards and almost wrap their arms around the horse's neck. If you do this and the horse suddenly swerves, stops or trips, you have little chance of staying on.

It is more than likely that a riding school horse will stop when he reaches his usual stopping place - if you really are in trouble, an escort should be making her way after you.

Whenever you ride you should wear protective headgear. Skull caps are strongly recommended, and carry the British Standards number 4472. Velvet caps should have a retaining harness secured on the shell at more than two points with the chinstrap properly adjusted and fastened. The BS number of these hats is 6473.

5
LEARNING TO JUMP

FOR SOME children, and indeed some adults, jumping is what riding is all about, with the preliminaries of walk, trot, canter, steering the horse and so on being something to get through as quickly as possible so the real fun can begin.

However, for the majority of adult beginners the process of learning to jump is often looked upon with some trepidation. Yet if everything is taken steadily there is no reason why jumping should not be great fun whatever your age. This skill also opens up whole new exciting worlds for you as a rider.

But how do you know when you can start jumping? Unfortunately, many people begin before they are actually ready and the result is that their introduction to jumping does not go as well as it should - the rider becomes nervous and thus finds everything that much more difficult. Work spent on developing your position will always pay off, so do not be in too much of a rush to start jumping. You really do need to have a secure, independent seat at walk, trot and canter first, and be able to steer confidently.

The jumping position

When a horse jumps he lengthens and elevates his stride. For small fences there is little elevation, but as the height increases so the horse has to make more effort and the degree of elevation increases.

As with all riding, it is vital that the rider stays in balance with the horse. On the flat the horse's centre of gravity lies just behind the withers, but as the animal jumps his centre of gravity moves forward as he stretches his head and neck forward. It makes sense therefore for the rider's position to move forward accordingly in order that she can stay in balance and harmony with the horse.

To achieve this forward or light seat the rider must first shorten her stirrup leathers, usually by a couple of holes. However, as your flatwork progresses and you achieve a deeper seat on the flat, you will need to shorten your leathers by a greater number of holes for jumping. The shortened leathers have the effect of moving your seat towards the back of the saddle so that the lower leg and knee can sit firmly around the horse. Your seat comes slightly out of the saddle and your body 'folds' down from the hips.

The size of the fence will dictate how much you need to fold. Keep a straight back and look ahead. The leg position should also be maintained while your elbows remain bent, and the hands must follow the movement of the horse's head. Your instructor will probably have you practising this position at halt, walk, trot and canter.

When you are capable of maintaining this position on the flat and in balance, you can try it out, first over poles and then small jumps. You may be provided with a neckstrap to hold on to so that you do not jab the horse in the mouth. Alternatively, hold on to the mane - this is preferable as your hands have to follow the movement of the horse's neck so you get the feel of how to allow for the horse stretching out his head and neck over a jump.

Trotting poles

Once you have practised your jumping position on the flat, your introduction to jumping will be via trotting poles. These may be placed on the ground at random or arranged in order, perhaps three in a row.

Initially you will walk over one pole, then trot, then work over three poles and possibly more. (Two poles should never be used as the horse may be tempted to jump them, thinking that it is a wide jump.) Aim for the centre of the pole, look up and try to keep the same walk or trot rhythm as you go over. You will be able to feel your horse look down at the poles and you need flexible elbows and arms to ensure that you do not restrict him.

Above left You will start to learn to jump by going over poles. Here our model is looking ahead and riding her pony forwards positively.

Left From a single pole you will progress to three or more, but do not ride any differently. Keep looking ahead and think of the trot rhythm. The poles are set at the correct distance for this pony - you can check this by looking at the footfalls, which should be in the middle of the distance between the poles.

Above Try to ride straight and at the centre of the poles. Here the pony is approaching too close to the left-hand side of the poles as seen by the rider.

If you are working as a ride, remember that you must keep the correct distance specified by your instructor. You should be able to turn away or ride past the poles if, for instance, a horse knocks them so that they are no longer at the correct distance.

To make life easier for the horse the poles will be set at 9 feet for walk and 4 feet 6 inches for trot. The distances vary according to the size of the horse and its stride - those quoted are for a 16-hands horse. Ideally the horse's footfalls will come down in the middle of the distance between each pole.

When working with poles:

- avoid letting the horse rush - think of the rhythm in your mind.

- avoid wiggling on the approach or get-away. Come in straight and go away from the poles straight.

- avoid resting on your hands - you cannot communicate properly with your horse if your hands are not in the correct position.

Whether you are working over poles or a jump (large or small) there are five phases to the jump. These are:

1 **The approach** - the horse should be given the best chance to meet the fence in the most suitable way. As a rider you need to think of bringing the horse in straight or on the best line possible, with plenty of impulsion (do not confuse this with speed) and with positive directions from you.

2 **The take-off** - the horse needs to lift his forehand, so you can imagine how much more difficult it is

for him if you are out of balance and too far forward. It is quite a common fault for riders to try and jump the fence in advance of their horse, or to try and lift the horse up with their hands - neither helps the animal. Be ready to follow the movement of the horse with your hands and arms but do not throw yourself forward.

There is a horsy saying about jumping: 'Throw your heart over first'. This is a fine mental attitude to adopt, but be careful that your body does not get too enthusiastic! You just need to fold forward - exaggerated movements will unbalance you and your horse.

3 **The flight** - this is when the horse will stretch his head and neck forward, particularly as the jump height increases, and you must allow the horse the freedom to do this and so balance himself. If you are left behind when the horse takes off and so are out of balance when he is in flight, you will affect the horse's jump - you may even cause him to bring a fence down!

4 **The landing** - the horse's forelegs extend, his head and neck will be raised and as his hindlegs come underneath him he makes. . .

5 **. . . the get-away.** It is important that you remain in balance while all this is going on - any wiggling on your part will show in the horse's behaviour. For instance, the horse may land on a back pole, may peck on landing or may be uncertain where he is supposed to go next.

Small jumps

Once you are happy going over trotting poles, your instructor will erect a small jump at the end of the poles, about 9 feet from the last pole. This jump will probably be a small crosspole - the cross helps to guide both horse and rider to the centre of the jump.

The trotting poles help you approach the fence in a good rhythm and all you need to do is keep looking ahead, keep your legs on the horse so he knows you mean to jump the fence, and be ready to follow his movement. Try to avoid the temptation to look down - remember that this will only unbalance your whole body and will certainly not help you to make a good attempt over the fence.

You will probably feel little elevation over a small jump, unless of course your mount is not too enthusiastic, loses his impulsion and has to make a real effort at the last minute, 'cat-jumping' instead of taking the fence smoothly in his stride.

Right The next step in jumping is to add a small cross pole at the end of the trotting poles. Our model has ridden in with plenty of activity so the pony can make a good jump. The cross guides both horse and rider to the centre of the fence.

Below right Whoops! This is what happens if the approach is wrong and the rider suddenly stops telling the pony that she wants to go forwards. You can see our rider's collapsed back, and she is looking down at the fence instead of where she wants to go - straight over it!

Once you have got the feel of going over a fence in trot, your instructor may remove the trotting poles and let you canter over a small crosspole, perhaps with a pole on the ground (known as a placing pole) positioned again about 9 feet in front of the jump. This enables the horse to meet the fence at the best possible place to take off and should provide you with a smooth jump.

When cantering towards a jump, concentrate on keeping a good canter rhythm, with plenty of impulsion, and let the fence come to you - that is, do not anticipate the jump, just sit, enjoy the canter and fold as you go over. Remember to sit up as you land so that you can keep the canter going - ideally you should keep the same rhythm before and after the fence.

Simple exercises can then be added to the jumping of a single fence. For instance, you may be asked to canter away left or right, to canter round to a certain point then trot, and so on.

Your single fence may be an upright or a spread, and if your instructor is an advocate of gridwork (also known as gymnastic jumping) you may find yourself building up to jumping several fences in a row. Gridwork is great for building up your sense of rhythm and feel, for teaching you to keep your legs on to help the horse jump the fences in the best possible way, and for improving your suppleness, balance and co-ordination.

Whatever you are doing, remember to look ahead, follow the horse's movement and keep telling him that you do want to jump the fences!

Above Next the trotting poles may be removed and just a placing pole used as shown here. The purpose of the placing pole is to help the horse meet the fence on a good stride so he can jump it well.

Left You can see how the rider has maintained a contact with the horse's mouth via the reins but has moved her hands up the horse's neck to allow him freedom of his head and neck. This freedom is vital for the horse so that he can balance himself.

Opposite Once you can cope with small single fences you may tackle a combination, in this case a double. It is important that the rider is supple and agile enough to pop the first fence and then be back in the saddle for the non-jumping stride between the two fences before going over the final element; note how the rider is looking well ahead.

Above You may then build up to a treble or a grid of fences, that is several fences in a row. You can see from this head-on shot how this rider puts more weight down through the right leg and looks left; this shift in balance will affect how the horse jumps.

Left This combination are gaining experience and having fun at a small show held at an equine centre. Many riding schools run fun events for their riders who can hire the school horses for a taste of competition.

Above right Once you are competent over small fences you can add to your experience by jumping into and over water, although not every riding school will have access to water jumps.

Right A nice secure lower leg from this rider as her horse jumps boldly into water.

Opposite Although this partnership have been together some time and have competed regularly they still have lessons over small grids to improve their skill, co-ordination and rhythm. You can see how the rider is keeping the weight down through the heels, is maintaining a flat back and is looking up.

This page Do not worry about jumping spread fences - you can see here how a horse can take a spread fence in her stride! Always be ready to allow your horse freedom over a fence, but do not give away the contact. You can see in the second photograph how the horse's near fore will be the first to hit the ground and will, for a split second, take the whole weight of horse and rider.

6
PROBLEMS AND SOLUTIONS

LEARNING to ride can take you a whole lifetime! You can, of course, master the basics in a much shorter time, but if you do continually want to improve, if you want to take on the challenge of getting the best out of every horse you ride, you will surely have a lifetime's learning ahead of you.

Along the route to mastering this riding business you will find many obstacles: there will be numerous occasions when you feel that you will never get the hang of a particular movement; when your legs seem to insist in moving backwards or forwards even though you are doing your best to keep them in one position; times when it seems that you just cannot 'ride' a particular horse.

Whether you are a novice rider or one with many years' experience under your belt, there are going to be times when you feel frustrated and as if your learning has reached a plateau with no chance of ever lifting off again.

It is during periods like this that your mental attitude to riding really comes into play. If you let negativity control you, it will not be long before the joys of riding are lost. You will soon give up and a whole world of challenge and enjoyment will be forfeited.

However, if you can just hold on and overcome your difficulties, a new and exciting phase of your riding career will soon begin. If riding was a simple art to master, there would be little reward in it: the fact that it can be difficult, demanding (both physically and mentally) and frustrating, just to mention a few of its challenges, means that the rewards, when they do come, are that much greater and more satisfying.

Riding is not for the faint-hearted, and by that I do not necessarily mean that you have to be exceedingly brave or bold. What you do have to be is tenacious and open-minded. When you hit a problem find out what is wrong (with the help of your instructor), work out a way of overcoming the difficulty, then set to in order to conquer your problem or fear, and get on with enjoying your riding.

In this chapter we will look at some of the common problems or worries novices come across, although many of these 'bad habits' can creep in to anyone's riding at any time, if the rider is not constantly on the alert and continually striving to improve.

Confidence

There are many reasons why a rider may lose confidence:

- poor tuition and therefore bad preparation for a particular riding task leading to poor execution and the rider feeling 'useless'

- a fall

- a frightening experience - being run off with, for example

- general lack of self-esteem

- being 'over-horsed' and unable to cope with the animal

- having lessons in a group where the overall group ability is higher so you are 'left behind' and feel incapable

- insensitive tuition, being 'bullied' into doing something you do not feel ready for

- peer pressure leading to an unhappy experience.

Whilst it is very easy to lose confidence - it takes only a few seconds - it can be a very long road to re-establish your belief in yourself and/or your horse. Many adults who are learning to ride start off with a confidence problem and it is vital that they seek

Falls are an inevitable part of a rider's life, and can easily shake your confidence if you let them

instruction from people who are sensitive to their particular needs.

Your riding should be enjoyable, and if it is not, you really must look at what is causing you distress. Is it the particular horse you are given to ride? Does one instructor instil you with fear? Are you happy with the riding school's safety precautions? You can always ask for a different horse, explain that you find instructor A much more helpful than B, or change riding schools if necessary.

Perhaps it is your general lack of skill that worries you and causes you to feel incapable and lacking in confidence? Why not invest in some lunge lessons instead of plugging on with the usual class lesson? The one-to-one tuition of a lunge lesson will prove invaluable in improving your riding position and therefore confidence; you will have the chance of building a rapport with a horse and with an instructor and there will be no other riders, coping better than you, to exert other pressure.

Another alternative is to find a good holiday centre (you will find advertisements for them in equestrian magazines) and have a concentrated week immersed in horses. The benefits will be tremendous - for a start you can concentrate solely on yourself instead of having to worry about getting to your lesson from work, fitting in the shopping and all those other routine hassles; you will be able to work on your riding problems from day to day instead of having a week for niggles and confidence-sappers to fester; the chance to have something explained by a different instructor, often throwing new light on a topic; and the satisfaction of being able to ride different horses and the chance to get away from your

usual surroundings. All this generally gives you the opportunity to put your riding into perspective.

Regaining confidence is not easy, but it will not happen at all unless you make it work. It's up to you to say 'I'm worried about so-and-so but I intend to conquer it'. Together with a sympathetic instructor and a reliable horse you can re-build your confidence. So whatever is bothering you, take the first steps *now* to get back on road to fun.

Controlling your nerves

Some people do not necessarily lack confidence, but their nerves can suddenly come into play so that they are unable to ride to the best of their ability at important times, for example when they are about to take an ABRS weekly rider's test, or make their first attempt at a BHS Horse Knowledge and Riding stage examination. Even the top riders have trouble with their nerves - often, if the adrenalin is not running, we do not give particularly good performances. Our nerves are a sign that what we are doing is important to us - if we did not care, then we probably would not be nervous.

Although anxiety in the right amount is beneficial, too much of it can create problems and leave us in the doldrums. You need to be able to use your anxiety in a positive way.

Many sportsmen and women now use the mental rehearsal technique before big matches or important games. Perhaps you are about to take your first ABRS test. Your instructor has run you through what is expected and you are as well prepared as you can be. You know what you have to do and that you are capable of doing it.

Going on a riding holiday will give you plenty of chance to enjoy new experiences and broaden your skills. The benefits of a week concentrating solely on yourself and your riding are immense, and may present you with different terrain and new challenges!

As the day draws near you have two choices. You could let yourself become increasingly worried by 'what if. . .' scenarios: 'What if I fall off, or can't remember how to check if I'm on the correct diagonal', etc, etc. If you follow this route you will soon be a gibbering wreck!

On the other hand you could adopt the mental rehearsal technique. Imagine it is 'the' day: you can visualise yourself mounting up with ease, executing smooth transitions, trotting wonderful 20 metre circles and smiling as the examiner announces that you have passed! Imagine every detail of your day, and see everything working out well. Keep these positive thoughts and scenes in your head and you will be amazed at the effect this rehearsal can have upon the real thing.

Some riders who are well practised at this mental rehearsal allow themselves to visualise making a mistake, but they also see how they would cope and correct the mistake. The benefit in this is that if something does go amiss, the rider is still prepared and has, through this mental rehearsal, prepared a contingency plan.

This technique can also be used to help you control your fears, of jumping perhaps, and put them into perspective. Naturally you will need to have some live practise of jumping as well, but visualising yourself popping over a fence with the greatest of ease has many more positive effects than letting a video of a nasty refusal or a horrendous fall keep playing across your mind.

Keeping in shape

In the early days of their riding career many people are surprised at how *physical* riding can be. As you progress and learn about the many subtleties of your chosen sport you will realise that you need to be fit to ride - you do not become fit for riding through riding alone.

You can employ some of the exercises mentioned elsewhere in this book to help your suppleness and muscle tone. Swimming is a good all-round exercise as well, whilst cycling will help your leg muscles. In short, the fitter you are, the easier your riding will be.

Body shape

It can be very easy to blame your lack of riding prowess on the fact that you are short, dumpy, or whatever. Whilst tall, slim riders do have a physical advantage, there are many good riders who do not fall into the 'ideal' body-shape category. Even the ideal people in terms of shape are not going to become good riders if they lack the will to learn, the

ability to feel what is happening with their horse or the open-mindedness so vital to a thinking rider.

Yes, your body shape may create problems for you - but they are not insurmountable! For example, short-legged riders may be tempted to lengthen their stirrups too much in an attempt to achieve a good length of leg. As a result their seats will be ineffective as they continually struggle to reach their stirrups. It is better to ride a little shorter and be effective than *look* okay but be unable to ride properly!

Mounting and dismounting

Initially this can seem to be an insurmountable obstacle! If you are a short but heavy person you may find that matters are even worse for you: in addition to the unfamiliar act of getting on and off your horse, you also have to cope with a larger horse because he is the only one who can carry your weight!

Whilst exercising and improving your muscle tone will help in the long term there is absolutely no reason why, in the short term, you should not use a mounting block. Most riding schools have one and a little improvisation can always come in useful. Do not be embarassed by the fact that you cannot haul yourself into the saddle. Children, fit eventers like Mark Todd and jockeys may be able to leap on to horses with consummate ease but, if the truth were known, most adults find it a bit of a chore!

Stiffness

This is the enemy of all riders, for it is inevitably accompanied by tension which makes life uncomfortable for both horse and rider. Suppling-up exercises will help - do some off the horse before you mount (one of my early instructors had everyone doing stretching exercises for a few minutes before they were allowed to mount up) and then spend the first few minutes on the horse carrying out simple exercises (see page 42 for ideas).

Stiffness and tension may also be brought about through the rider's fear or lack of confidence - so you need to address these aspects as well.

A better position

Rising and sitting trot

All novice riders go through a phase of being unable to do anything other than bounce around, totally out of rhythm with the trot and feeling mighty uncomfortable. The good news is that this phase will pass!

When you are learning to ride and trying to sit to the trot, you often find yourself gripping up with your legs so that you bounce around even more; you are alsothrown forward, which feels very unsafe, and it is

Seat savers are a great bonus if you suffer from saddle soreness - they can quickly and easily be fitted on to your saddle before a weekly riding lesson.

impossible to keep your hands from behaving as though you are conducting an orchestra, no matter how much you try to obey your instructor's commands.

One way to get through this difficult stage with the minimum of fuss and the maximum benefit to you is to have lunge lessons. Depending on the riding school, you may have several initial lunge lessons before being allowed 'off the lunge' and into class lessons. Hopefully this will really give you a firm grounding as far as your position is concerned and the mastery of the trot.

However, many riding schools get people into class lessons as quickly as possible, as clients often feel that they are not making progress unless they are moving under their own steam as opposed to being on the lunge.

If you can control your ego and commit yourself to some lunge lessons early in your riding education they will, if properly conducted, provide you with a solid base which will reap dividends in the future. Spend time working on the foundations of your riding, right from the very early days, and you will save yourself time and expense later, because it is much harder to erase bad habits than it is to instil good ones at the beginning. By undertaking exercises on the lunge, on a comfy horse that has smooth, even paces, you will soon master the art of rising and sitting trot.

Trot and canter

Another common problem for new riders is getting the horse into a trot or canter and then maintaining it. Often the difficulty lies in poor preparation and then bad application of the aids.

If the pace before the required one is bad, the new pace will be poor too. To move into trot, the horse must first be walking on actively, paying attention to the rider. Tune in to how your horse feels. Is he marching out in walk as if he is going places? Or does it feel as if each step is his last and he is going to grind to a halt at the earliest opportunity? If your horse needs waking up, get after him - and if he does not respond to your leg aids, then use your stick to back up the leg and remind the horse that he is to obey instructions.

For canter transitions you must remember that the trot needs to be *active* - which is different from *fast*. You often see novice riders rushing around on horses that are trotting flat out but cannot move up a gear into canter. If you look sideways on at a horse that is rushing in trot you can see that the animal's whole frame is long and strung out. As a result the hindlegs are not coming underneath the body particularly well. When the trot is active and the rider has control of the pace, the horse's frame is more rounded and his hindlegs will come further under his body. This makes it easier for the horse to move up a gear and to push off into canter (remember that it is a hindleg that starts the canter sequence).

Once you have an active trot you must remember to sit to the trot before you ask the horse for canter. Check too that your position is as good as it possibly can be and that you are giving the correct aids. It makes life easier for your horse if you ask him to canter in a corner.

Maintaining the canter can be just as difficult for some new riders as getting the pace in the first place. Keep to the forefront of your mind the thought that your legs must always be 'on' the horse. Unless your legs are there, engaging the horse in conversation and saying 'go', your mount will not know what is required of him.

The balance of the amount of the rider's leg to the amount of hand is a difficult equation, and not just at the lower levels of riding. Beginners who are stiff in the arms and therefore have restrictive hands will find that their fault magnifies as the horse moves faster. In canter the horse moves his head and therefore the rider's hands have to move with the horse in order to maintain a good even contact and allow the horse freedom to move. Any restriction in the rider's hands will be felt by the horse, and if restrictive hands are also coupled with legs that are not applying enough pressure, the rider will have difficulty in maintaining the canter.

Work on the lunge without stirrups or without reins (you are recommended to always have one or the other when being lunged) and work without stirrups off the lunge will improve your position, deepen your seat and make you more independent, all of which will assist your canter and their riding work generally.

Other common canter problems such as perching forwards, looking down to check strike-off, leaning back and bouncing around, can all be helped through work on the lunge.

Looking down and slouching

As one instructor said, 'There are no instructions on the horse's neck, so stop looking for them!'. Looking down is a fault we can all easily slip into, and it is a bad one which has implications for other elements of our position as well.

The head is a relatively heavy part of our body and by looking down we put the whole of our upper body out of balance. This in turn puts greater weight on the horse's forehand and makes it more difficult for him to carry us.

If you are looking down you cannot see potential hazards looming ahead and are thus unable to forestall any difficulties. Once you start jumping, looking down into the bottom of the fence tends to result in the horse putting on the brakes at the last minute -

Ask a friend to video you or take photographs. Studying them can give you a better idea of your riding position and how it might be improved.

and, of course, there is also the saying that where you look is where you end up!

An associated fault with looking down is slouching of the shoulders - it is difficult to do anything but when your head is drooping. This affects the whole carriage of your upper body and has a direct influence on how effectively or otherwise you can use your aids to control and guide your horse.

Self-discipline is the key to solving this problem - you have to constantly think and correct yourself. Slouching is probably a habit that extends outside your riding too - as you sit at your office desk, or in the car, or at home, just stop and take stock of your posture. Work at improving it now - you will feel better and the picture you present, whether on horseback or not, will have more elegance and command more attention.

Something the Army does with its riders is have them carry a short stick across their back, between their arms. This means the riders have to sit tall, with their shoulders back and their arms in the correct position - no slouching allowed here!

Often if you have a tendency to slouch and look down, your hands also drop lower than the advised position. Remember the straight line from the horse's mouth through the rein to the hand, wrist and elbow of the rider? This position enables the rider to follow the movement of the horse's head sympathetically; if this line is broken by the rider's hands being too low, the rider's hand will also be stiffer and more restrictive, all of which will be felt by the horse's sensitive mouth.

Gripping up
No matter how you try, have you got legs that insist on riding upwards? It is a common fault - everyone who has ever ridden will have experienced it at some point.

Achieving a 'long, relaxed leg' which remains in the correct position, moulded to the horse's side, ready to apply aids as necessary, takes a great deal of practice.

Lunge lessons will again prove invaluable. However, they will be of no benefit if the horse is allowed to rush on, so it is important to select a school where lungeing is a regular activity and where there are suitable horses and instructors. There is a definite art to lungeing a horse and rider, so choose your centre carefully.

Lack of rhythm
If you watch a group of people dancing it is obvious that some have much more natural rhythm than others. This also shows up when you ride, which is why some people have real trouble mastering rising trot whilst others take to it as if they were born in the saddle.

Repeating the rhythm in your head or out loud helps. If you are really struggling, your instructor could call out the rhythm and you only need to concentrate on tuning in! Some people find it beneficial to hum or sing to themselves, whilst others find riding to music helps (although of course the songs have to be carefully selected). There are a number of dressage riders who give dressage-to-music demonstrations, and it is worth going along to one of these if you need a few ideas about music selection.

Again, lunge lessons will help develop your feel for what is happening to the horse underneath you.

Out of balance
For the horse, carrying an out-of-balance rider is a real chore. It is just like you giving a friend a piggy back when they decide to sway about in a drunken manner! The only way a rider can become in balance is to have

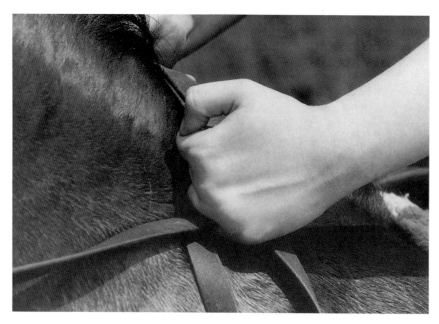

How to bridge the reins - a useful technique if a horse pulls, so that you are not dragged forward or lose the rein contact.

concentrated instruction so that you are really established in your riding position (the position is designed to be the most effective one for the horse to be able to carry himself and you in balance). This will of necessity mean work both on and off the lunge, and a great deal of effort and self-discipline from the rider.

Collapsing hips/shoulders

A rider may have poor posture before she even gets on a horse, so that once mounted she does not even notice that one side of her body tends to collapse as she executes turns or circles. Even riders who seem pretty even off a horse, collapse on one side when mounted. This shift of weight will influence the horse and the problem of unevenness needs to be addressed or you will always create problems for yourself and any horse you ride.

Your instructor should point out the problem to you - or you may notice it yourself if you see photographs of yourself or have the chance to be videoed when riding. Some schools do have mirrors in their indoor schools, which assists greatly as you can see whether you are sitting askew or not. Once you are aware of the problem, you need self-discipline to help you constantly check and correct yourself.

Better jumping

Many jumping difficulties stem from the rider's lack of ability, or a lack of confidence to 'throw their heart over first'. If your introduction to jumping has been properly conducted, you should see this branch of riding as an exciting and enjoyable challenge; if your preparation has been poor you can dread the sight of a fence! If lack of ability is the problem, there is no substitute for stepping back, returning to basics and building a solid foundation before you try jumping again. Then you can practice, under instruction, and jumping should become fun.

Confidence

Maybe you have experienced a nasty fall - or the thought of one is enough to make you baulk at the idea of jumping. If a lack of confidence is the problem, you really need to sit down and decide just what you want to do. Some people never leave the ground yet they have a satisfying riding career, seeking their challenges elsewhere, such as in the dressage arena or the long-distance riding field. Many hundreds of thousands of people are content simply to ride around the countryside.

To some folk, however, the idea of not jumping is anathema. Whatever happens they get back on and carry on - the pleasure of sailing over cross-country fences or pitting their wits against a course builder outweighs the tumbles. Such people find it hard to believe that anyone could not want to jump fences.

The most important question is: what do *you* want? Not your instructor, or your partner, or your riding companion, but *you*! Will your enjoyment of riding suffer if you never go near a fence again? Are you determined to fulfil a long-held ambition of riding in a riding club's one-day event? Are you prepared to conquer your fear? Or do you want to redirect your energies into a different, but just as challenging, branch of equestrianism? The decision has to be yours, because if you are to overcome a lack of confidence where jumping is concerned, other people can help but they cannot get inside your head and provide the determination when the going gets tough. Your commitment is essential whether you suffer a confidence crisis as a newcomer to riding, or as an old hand. The height of the fences may differ, but the scale of the problem is just as great.

If you have made the decision to conquer your fear of jumping then practice, practice, practice. You will need the help of a sympathetic instructor and a steady, reliable horse - but you must get out there and jump fences. Start off over trotting poles, then add a fence, work through small grids and gradually build up. If you can, arrange for a series of lessons on consecutive days, you will find progress is usually much quicker. Set yourself goals each day, and talk to your instructor so you also know what plan of action she has. Sometimes worrying about what height the fences will go to today is such a soul-destroying exercise that you have no energy for anything else.

Give yourself a pat on the back when you achieve your goals - they may seem like small steps to other people, but you know how big an obstacle you have overcome. Be kind to yourself and recognise your good points, and before you know it, you will be well on the way to popping fences confidently.

Refusals and run-outs

Sometimes you want to jump a fence but you never seem to get it right - the horse either refuses point blank or runs out at the last second.

The majority of jumping problems are caused by the rider, not the horse. Being determined to jump a fence is not enough - you also have to make the horse's task as easy as possible. So, if you do not create enough impulsion or you bring the horse into the fence on a difficult angle, then it is likely the horse will stop or run out. So when you are jumping, think before you launch yourself at a fence:

● Do you have an active pace from the horse? Your instructor will no doubt tell you whether

If the approach is wrong, the rider invites a horse to misbehave.

she expects you to approach the fence in trot or canter but it is up to you to establish an active, forward-going pace. Remember that this does not mean speed! If you are working in canter the horse's hindlegs need to be coming well under his body - take a look at the pictures on pages 56-7 illustrating an active, rounded canter and a flatter, less active one.

● In order to maintain this activity you need to ensure that your legs are constantly giving the horse friendly nudges, letting him know that you intend keeping up this rhythm as you jump the fence.

● Your contact will also need to be good - remember that while initially you will have been taught to jump using a fairly loose rein, once you are more practised you should be riding the horse into a decent contact, with plenty of leg.

● How you present the horse at the fence is important. Apart from riding him with plenty of impulsion, you also need to remember to steer so you have a straight approach and aim for the centre of the fence. Remember to turn towards a fence in plenty of time (short turns into fences and jumping on the angle are for when you are a more experienced rider working towards competition success).

● Look for your turn and your fence in plenty of time. However, do not sight on to the fence and then allow your eyes to wander to the base of the fence. Look up and away, over the fence.

● Avoid any temptation to fiddle with your horse in the final three strides before the fence. If you have not got everything right by now it is too late anyway.

● Concentrate on thinking of your trot or canter rhythm rather than making a big thing of the fence in front of you.

● Beware of letting your hip or shoulder collapse - try to sit square. If you do have a tendency to collapse to one side on approach, you are encouraging the horse to take advantage and duck out to that side.

● Try not to anticipate the fence, standing up in your stirrups as your horse takes off. Remember to fold down, letting your weight sink through your knees and ankles.

● If you find that your lower legs sail backwards over a fence this is because you are tipping on to your knees, rather than letting your weight go down *through* your knees.

● Perhaps you find yourself getting left behind every time the horse jumps? You can improve your suppleness and your sense of timing by working through a grid (series of fences).

If your riding school does not offer particularly good tuition as far as jumping is concerned, it is worth finding somewhere that does. Otherwise you could spend a long time struggling and the only result will be that your confidence and riding ability suffers.

7
WHAT NEXT?

WITH THE rudiments of riding on the flat and over fences mastered there is bound to come the point when you would like more involvement with horses than your usual weekly lesson. If this is the case, there are endless possibilities. Most of the options given here will give you a good grounding if you do decide to take the next step and buy your own horse. At the worst, they will bring you into contact with other horsy people and widen your circle of friends.

Some of the activities are riding-school based, others will take you into the wider horse world.

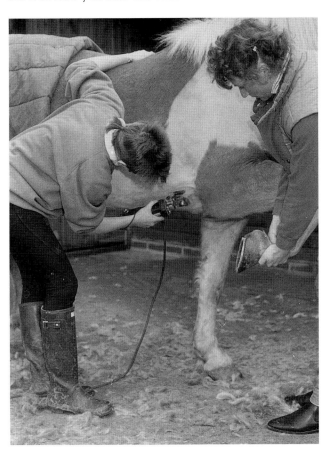

Tests and certificates

ABRS Weekly Riders' Tests
If your school is ABRS approved, your instructor will be able to tell you about this series of tests which provides a structure for your weekly riding progress and gives you something positive to work to. Another advantage of these tests is that they are very inexpensive but do provide a goal and a reward for weekly riders. Successful candidates are awarded certificates and, of course, you can prepare for and take the exam at your riding school.

British Horse Society Horse Owners Certificates
If you are considering owning a horse, it would be well worth your while to train for these certificates. Ideally they should be undertaken before you commit yourself to horse ownership as they will prepare you for the rigours of life with horses.
There are three levels:

Level 1 deals with subjects such as horse colours, markings and uses; elementary stable management; stable safety; recognition of and basic care of tack; grooming; recognising ill health; when to call a vet; preventative treatments; principles of watering and feeding; knowledge of buying a horse; preparing a horse for a ride; post-ride care; riding on the roads and riding dress.

Level 2 includes reasons for shoeing; recognising when shoeing is needed; common injuries and first aid; watering and feeding of the horse at grass and the stabled horse; grassland maintenance; care of sad-

If you do not have a horse of your own, offer your services to owners - it's a great chance to learn about so many aspects of horsy life.

Left Before you become a horse owner it is a good idea to take the British Horse Society Horse Owner's Certificate. This will involve learning how to look after a horse in all seasons and circumstances.

Below far left The importance of proper shoeing should not be underestimated. This poor pony's feet have been allowed to become grossly overgrown. Neglect like this often happens through ignorance.

Below left Take any chance to watch a farrier at work - many are only too happy to explain what they are doing, which is valuable information.

dlery; insurance; stable routine; bedding; the Highway and Country Codes.

Level 3 looks at the recognition, treatment and care of common injuries and ailments; management changes when a horse is turned out to grass/ brought in from grass; plaiting, trimming and clipping; care and maintenance of horse transport; the law concerning the transit of the horse; preparing a horse for travel; care of the horse for competitive events and trekking; fitness and condition - an understanding of them and maintenance of both; stable construction; layout of stable yards, siting of the muck heap and its disposal; horse clothing and bandaging; recognising good and bad forage, and storage of forage; knowledge of costs and of the activities of the BHS, Riding Clubs and Pony Club.

As you can see, these are comprehensive and would stand you in good stead for horse ownership. The tests are run by approved BHS riding schools and by local authorities, for instance college evening classes. The tests are theoretical, taking the form of a written exam lasting one and a half hours. Candidates of all ages have taken the tests - you can find out more from the Training and Examinations Office at the British Horse Society (tel 0203 696697).

Certificate of Competence in Horsekeeping

Aware that future European Community directives may include the necessity for horse owners to hold a suitable formal qualification, the Riding Clubs Movement has, in conjunction with the National Proficiency Tests Council, developed a new Certificate of Competence in Horsekeeping.

The Certificate comprises two separate units - Animal Welfare and Health & Safety of People - both of which must be passed. The Animal Welfare unit requires a knowledge of:

- Acts of Parliament that protect the horse

- feeding and watering
- recognition of ill health in the horse
- when to call the vet
- the feet and shoeing
- parasite control
- common diseases
- vaccinations

The second unit requires an understanding of the dangers involved in handling horses. As the required standards for the scheme and the desired answers are all published in advance, candidates simply have to show that they have understood and absorbed the information. Their chance to demonstrate this is via a written test lasting about an hour and a short 'hands-on' practical session as well.

Anyone can take the test - you do not have to belong to a Riding Club - but access to the scheme is likely to be via riding clubs, riding establishments and colleges running equestrian courses. For more information contact the Riding Clubs Office at the BHS or the National Proficiency Tests Council, National Agricultural Centre, Stoneleigh, Kenilworth, Warks, CV8 2LG (tel 0203 696553).

BHS Horse Knowledge and Riding Stages examinations

These exams are very much regarded as the professional qualifications of the BHS as they are taken, in conjunction with teaching qualifications, by people wishing to pursue careers as instructors. (You can see from page 12 which stages relate to which instructional exam.) However, these exams are open to riders over the age of 17, and they can provide a useful measure of your riding and stable management skills.

Of the exams we have mentioned so far, these are the most expensive to take, and you would be well advised to work for these examinations in conjunction with courses at a riding school or with a freelance instructor.

It is not just the knowledge but also the exam technique that is important - and you must be able to ride a selection of horses. Preparation for these exams is also available part-time at many colleges or as 'holiday' breaks at riding schools.

ABRS qualifications

In addition to their weekly riders' tests, the ABRS have their own professional qualifications, including a teaching one, which are very practically based. You will need some full time experience of working with

Plaiting manes is a skill required for some practical horse care examinations.

horses - but if you get a severe dose of the horse bug and do consider making a career with horses, you would be sensible to investigate the ABRS qualifications.

Correspondence courses

Equestrian magazines carry advertisements for home-based equestrian courses - some leading to BHS exams, others aimed at self-improvement. These can be quite expensive for the material, but they do enable you to learn at your own pace and are ideal for people living too far from the usual equestrian centres or colleges or resident in very remote areas.

So far, the options have been very goal-orientated and formal - but of course there is a great deal to be learned, and considerable fun to be had, from being involved with horses on a less competitive level.

Helping out at your riding school

One way to gain experience of caring for horses is to see if your riding school encourages people to help out on the yard. Some smaller ones would not be able to function efficiently at busy times without unpaid help from willing people, whereas other centres prefer not to have too many people milling around the yard. They may well offer stable management lessons and although these are a good starting point, there is no substitute for actual, practical experience.

If you are able to lend a hand on the yard, here are some of the tasks you may be asked to undertake along with a suggested way of undertaking them:

Filling water buckets and haynets

Horses should have fresh clean water available to them at all times so a regular part of the yard routine will be checking the water supply. Some yards will keep clean water buckets near the tap; fill these and then go around the stables, topping up the stable buckets as required. However, at least once a day the water buckets should be removed from the stables, emptied and scrubbed clean before being refilled.

Your school may feed hay in a variety of ways - in nets, on the floor or in racks. Whatever the method, each horse or pony will be allocated a certain amount of hay at certain times during the day, for example morning, lunchtime, late afternoon and at evening stables. If haynets are to be filled, ensure that the hay is thoroughly shaken before it is placed in the net. A spring measure should be available somewhere near the hay supply so that the amount of hay can be measured. Often a system operates so that all the 9-pound nets are put in one place, the 6-pound nets somewhere else, and so on.

Ensure that unwanted baler twine from the hay bales is put away - often a sack is kept for this purpose near the hay store.

If you tie a haynet in the stable, ensure that it is tied with a quick release knot and hung sufficiently far off the ground so that when empty there is no danger of the horse catching his feet in the net.

Cleaning out feed bowls

Although the feeding will probably be carried out by whoever runs the yard, you can always assist at feed times by handing out feeds, collecting bowls and washing them out.

The yard manager should warn you of any horses with peculiar habits at feed times, but always enter a stable with quiet assurance. Horses will realise if you are nervous of them. Remember to speak before you approach and ensure that you do not let the horse escape as you open the stable door. Deliver any feed into the manger without letting the horse thrust his nose into the bowl on the way.

Feed bowls should be thoroughly washed out - you would not want bits of food left on your plate for days on end, so treat the horse's feeding utensils with the same respect.

Skipping out

Well-kept yards will operate a regular 'skipping out' programme. This means that droppings and soiled patches are removed from the horse's beds at regular intervals through the day. This not only keeps the stable cleaner and sweeter but ensures that the horse is not soiling himself by lying down on droppings. It also gives a much better impression for people coming on to the yard.

Whenever you skip out, take the chance to check the horse's water supply as well. If the stable is fitted with an automatic watering system this can easily be blocked up if the horse has deposited some droppings into the bowl.

Mucking out

The major mucking out, or cleaning, of the horse's stable is generally carried out in the morning. If you help at a yard you will probably be shown how they like you to muck out, but here's a rough guide to dealing with a stable:

1 Collect together mucking-out tools, ie wheelbarrow, fork, shovel, brush.
2 Put headcollar on horse and tie him up, inside the stable if necessary or outside if that is possible. Remove water bowls.
3 Remove all visible droppings from the bed.
4 Systematically, working from one corner, lift all the bedding, throwing wet and soiled bedding into the wheelbarrow and putting dry and reusable bedding up against one of the stable walls.
5 When all the bedding has been sorted and the dry bedding is against one wall, brush the stable floor. It is advisable to leave the bedding up for a while so that the stable floor can dry and air. However, this may not be feasible if the horse has to stay in the box. In this case, put the bed down again, adding new bedding as required to give a good, deep bed.
6 Fork test - if the bed is deep enough, when you stick your fork into it you should not be able to see the prongs. If you can see the prongs then more bedding is needed.
7 Replace water bowls and return the horse to its box or untie him as the case may be.
8 Sweep the area outside the stable door so that everywhere is clean and tidy.
9 Dispose of unwanted bedding on the muck heap (often more than one trip is needed per stable).
10 Tidy up the muck heap and then return stable tools to their place.

Tidying the yard

This is a thankless but essential task. A tidy yard gives a good impression, but more importantly it is also a safe place.

Helpers for mucking out are generally welcomed by riding schools. Note how the dry, reusable bedding is being piled against the wall.

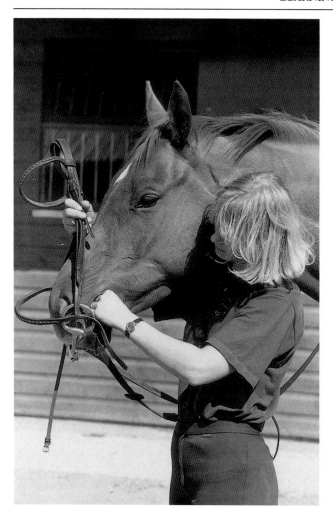

Tacking up is a skill you can practise when helping out at your local riding school. The left hand is being used to open the corner of the horse's mouth, while the right hand takes the bridle up towards the offside ear.

It is vital that all tools are kept in a safe place; if left around they are inviting accidents to people and horses. With so much material around that could easily catch fire, such as hay and straw, it makes sense to keep a litter-free, tidy yard. If everywhere is a mess then clients may feel it is quite okay to drop litter and cigarette ends!

Tacking up

Once you know the horses and how to tack up, you can be a great help in preparing animals for lessons. The tackroom should be organised so that each horse's saddle, bridle and any accessories such as boots or martingales are clearly marked with the animal's name.

It is usual for tacked-up animals to be left tied up in their stalls or stables - if left loose they may roll and damage their saddles, or get their legs caught up in reins, etc. Check that the horse is clean - especial-

ly where the tack will come into contact with his skin. It may be necessary for you to remove mud or sweat marks before tacking up. If you do not, you run the risk of the horse getting sores.

Before you tack up, go in, put a headcollar on the horse and tie him up. Stand on the horse's nearside and put the reins over his head; then undo the headcollar, slip it off the horse's head and secure it around his neck so he cannot go anywhere. Bring your right arm under the horse's jaw so you can steady his head with your right hand. With your right hand take hold of the bridle, about half way up, and with your left hand take hold of the bit. Slip the thumb of your left hand into the corner of the horse's mouth and slide the bit in, taking the rest of the bridle up so that you can slip the horse's offside ear into the bridle with your right hand, then place the bridle over the nearside ear. Take the forelock over the browband, check that the browband is not pinching at the horse's ears, then fasten the throatlash (winding the reins around and securing them with the throatlash) and noseband. Replace the headcollar.

Now to the saddle - check the stirrup irons are run up and the girth is over the top of the saddle. Place the saddle in front of the horse's withers at the nearside and slide it back into position. Check that any numnah or saddle cloth being used is not ruffled up, then attach the girth to the offside and do the girth up on the nearside. Do not tighten the girth ready for riding but have it sufficiently secure so that the saddle does not slip.

Tack cleaning

Ideally a horse's tack should be cleaned every day, especially if it has been used several times during the day. At the very least, each time a bridle is used the bit should be washed off. Some schools are able to strip down the tack (that is, take it apart completely, removing stirrup irons, girths, bits, etc, as well as taking apart all leatherwork) daily and clean it, but more often than not a thorough strip down will be a once a week job. Daily cleaning will involve wiping the dirt and grease off, then saddle soaping whilst the tack is still complete.

If you do take the tack apart, do remember which holes the various pieces are on. As riding schools may have to make bridles up out of odd pieces here and there, it is quite likely that the cheekpieces on a bridle will be two different lengths.

Use a damp sponge to remove dirt and grease, taking care not to get the tack too wet. If some greasy patches are particularly difficult to remove, get some horse hair, wind it into a ball and use this to remove the grease.

Once all the leather is clean it can be soaped. There

are various types of leather care products from the straightforward bars of glycerine saddle soap to costly preparations. Be careful not to create a lather with the soap - ensure your sponge is dampish, not wet. Wipe over both sides of the leatherwork, not just the side you see. It is the side next to the horse which tends to dry out and therefore needs to be replenished.

Make sure the bit is cleaned with warm water and dried. Stirrup irons can be immersed in water and the muck scrubbed off. If the girth is very dirty it may need washing and drying.

Once everything has been soaped, reassemble the tack and give it a final wipe over with the sponge before hanging it up. Ensure any numnahs are removed and stored so that the side which comes into contact with the horse can be aired and dried. Numnahs and saddle cloths also need to be washed regularly.

Turning horses out

If your school lets its animals have time out at liberty, you can assist with turning the horses out. Some horses can become rather strong when being led out to grass, so these are led out in bridles as opposed to headcollars. Anyone who asks you to help should brief you on what the procedure is for any particular horse.

If the animal is difficult to catch it may have its headcollar left on - check before you turn anything out if this is the case. Horses that are left with headcollars on ought to be turned out in leather headcollars; this is because leather will break if the horse gets entangled anywhere, whereas nylon will not and serious injuries can result.

If more than one animal is being turned out into a field, all the horses should be taken into the field and the gate closed before any are set free. It is sensible to release all the horses at the same time or you may find yourself with an animal going loopy because its friend has just shot off around the corner and you have not made any attempts to release it yet!

Always turn the horse towards the field gate before you release him - this should ensure that you do not get kicked by flying hooves if the horse disappears off at a great pace.

Turning out horses is a task which will help build your handling skills.

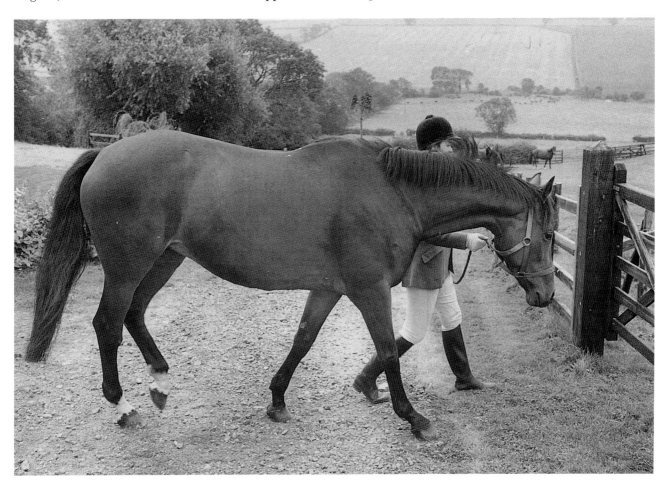

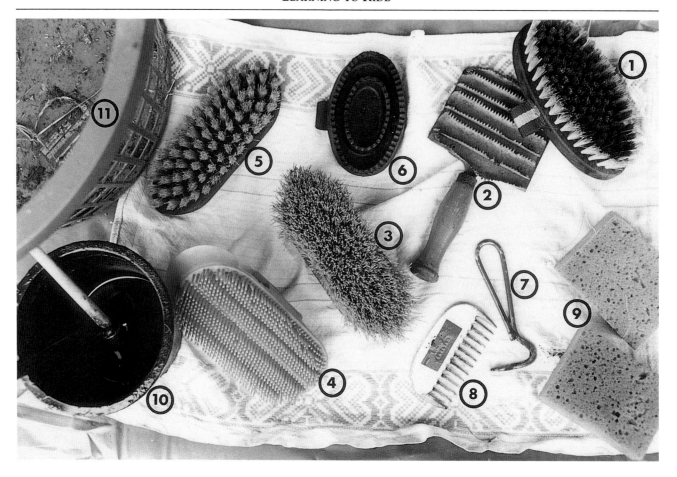

Essential equipment: 1 Body brush, 2 Metal curry comb, 3 Dandy brush, 4 Plastic curry comb, 5 Water brush, 6 Rubber curry comb, 7 Hoofpick, 8 Tail comb, 9 Sponges, 10 Hoof oil, 11 Skip.

Grooming

This is an important part of every horse's daily routine. Apart from making the horse look cleaner and smarter, it is vital for health, ensuring that the horse's circulation is stimulated, that dead cells are removed, and that muscle tone and the coat condition are improved. It also provides a chance to check the horse over for any injuries, cuts, swelling or unaccustomed heat (in the legs, for example, which may mean that the horse has strained himself and is lame).

The conditions under which the animal is kept will determine the type and amount of grooming. For example, ponies kept out at grass will not have such a thorough grooming as it is not desirable to remove too many of the natural oils from their coats, which are needed to give protection against the elements. Horses which are sick will only need the briefest of freshening up to make them comfortable.

Quartering is the name given to the type of grooming that is carried out before a horse is ridden. Basically this involves brushing the horse over quickly so that tack can be fitted without fear of causing rubs and sores, the feet are then picked out and the eyes/nostrils/dock wiped clean.

Once the horse has been exercised, his pores are open and a thorough grooming (known as strapping) is more beneficial. Strapping takes around 45 minutes to do properly. These are the jobs involved:

• Pick out the feet, taking the opportunity to check the wear of the shoe, whether any clenches have risen or if it is loose. Using a hoofpick, work from heel to toe, removing dirt from the lateral clefts of the frog and, very carefully, from the central cleft.

• Remove any mud with the help of a dandy brush or a rubber curry comb. The latter is also useful for removing loose hairs when the horse is changing coats - use the comb in a circular motion.

• To really clean the coat a body brush is used (this has softer, shorter bristles than a dandy brush and gets well down into the coat). Always brush with the lie of the coat, putting

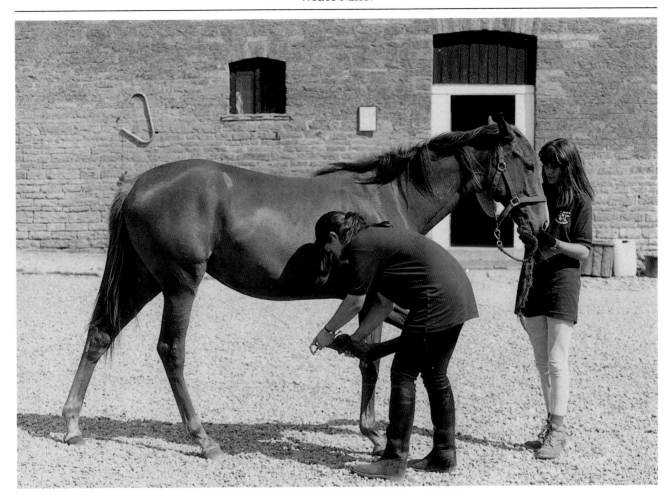

When picking out the horse's feet, take the opportunity to check the condition of the shoes.

the weight of your body behind each stroke with the body brush. Every few strokes, clean the body brush by pulling a metal curry comb across it.

● Work from the head, being careful with the use of the brush around the horse's head. Some are very wary around their heads and need sympathetic but firm handling. A soft cloth may be used instead of a brush until the horse becomes more accustomed to having his head handled.

● The body brush is also used on the mane and tail - although if the horse has very fine hairs you may find it preserves his mane and tail if you carefully use your fingers to separate the hairs. Do not use a dandy brush on these areas as it will break the hairs.

● A water brush may be used to dampen the mane and ensure it lays over to the correct side of the neck (ie the offside).

● Untangle the tail - a little baby oil rubbed into it will help here.

● To help the tail keep its shape, you can bandage it. Dampen the tail hairs at the top of the tail to lay them down (but do not dampen the bandage as, being elastic, it can shrink and place undue pressure on the tail). Tail bandages must never be left on overnight or for long periods or damage to the tail can ensue.

● Once the horse is thoroughly cleaned he can be 'wisped'. This entails using a wisp made of hay or a leather pad, which is brought down upon the muscles of the neck and hindquarters to improve their tone. Never wisp the horse on his loins as this is a weak area of his back.

● Use a clean damp sponge to wipe around the horse's eyes and nostrils. With a separate damp sponge wipe around the dock, teats or sheath.

● The final act is to add hoof polish and wipe the horse over with a stable rubber to remove the last of any dust.

Meeting people

The riding clubs movement

Throughout Britain there are clubs that offer training, shows, fun competitions and social events to horsy people. A large number of people who belong to riding clubs are horse-owners, but non-owners are just as welcome, especially if they are prepared to get involved in show organisation, etc.

Apart from the chance to meet local riders, this gives you the opportunity to learn a great deal about riding and the various competition rules. For instance, acting as a writer for a dressage judge will improve your understanding of a horse's paces, his outline and acceptance of the bit as well as how to execute dressage movements correctly.

Assisting as a steward in a showing class will improve your eye for a horse and the way horses move, while helping to build show jumping courses gives you the chance to understand the logic behind a course and the problems that are presented to the horse and rider.

Social activities organised by the club will widen your circle of friends and it is possible that you will find an owner who needs assistance with her horse. As so many people have to work to keep their horses, there is not always the time to do everything, so a competent helper who could perhaps hack the horse out one evening a week is a godsend. Rides tend to come via personal contact so start getting to know people!

Riding holidays

There are some terrific holidays on offer - and not just based in Britain either! Whether you want to ride across Scotland, go bed-and-breakfasting with a horse in Wales, taste the cowboy life in America, experience the thrill of race meetings in France, or have a go at hunting in Ireland, there are many possibilities.

Equestrian magazines carry advertisements and occasionally reviews of horsy holidays. Look for the ones that members of the staff have tried themselves if possible. Keep away from holidays that are extremely cheap - to keep good horses in good condition so that they can work six hours a day crossing difficult terrain is not cheap, so a good trail-riding centre will have to make a sensible charge. The same applies to providing good instructional weeks on suitable horses.

Shows

There is a great deal to be learned from just spectating at shows - and if you can get to some of the bigger events, an hour or so spent watching top riders work in their horses for dressage, showjumping, etc, is extremely enlightening.

Riding for other people

Personal contact may bring the offer of rides - for instance to help an expectant mum who is reluctant to sell her horse but needs someone to exercise it during her pregnancy, or to fill in while an owner is away at college or whilst the usual rider is working away, and so on.

If you do start riding for other people it is as well to have your own insurance cover (some companies

Wherever you live there are opportunities to be involved with horses.

do rider-only insurance policies) and to be a member of the BHS so you have some public liability cover too. Do not take it for granted that a horse will be insured by its owner. Do make sure that you and the owner discuss, in advance, and commit to paper, exactly what the arrangement will be: when you will ride; whether you are expected to pay for the ride; if so, how much; if not, are you expected to perform stable duties?; what happens if the horse injures itself while ridden by you? Think of the worst possible scenarios and get answers so you, and the horse's owner, know exactly where you each stand.

If you decide to take a horse on loan it is even more important to get a suitable contract drawn up. *Your Horse* magazine has published such contracts in the past and will offer you help and advice on this matter. For a copy of the contract, send an sae to *Your Horse* magazine, Bretton Court, Bretton, Peterborough, PE3 8DZ (please remember to state what it is you want!).

Points you must cover are the duration of the loan period; who is responsible for insuring the horse; who is responsible for veterinary bills (including routine vaccinations and teeth rasping); what activities the horse may or may not do; where the horse is to be kept; amount of notice required either way; which farrier and vet are to be used; any special requirements of the horse; whether there is an option to buy; and access arrangements for the owner (presuming that the horse is kept away from the owner's premises).

There is more about taking a horse on loan in Part 2, but for now be aware of the advantages and disadvantages. The disadvantages are:

● You are investing time and money into someone else's horse and they may curtail the loan at relatively short notice.

● You are unlikely to get anything back for your investment other than the satisfaction of riding the horse. It can be galling if you really improve a horse and the owners then sell it on, making a reasonable profit for themselves while you have nothing left to ride!

● It is not a pleasant job telling an owner if a misfortune happens to the horse while in your care.

● You can develop a good partnership with the horse but it may then be sold from underneath you.

● Although an option-to-buy clause is sensible, an owner could still set the price of the horse at an unreasonably high level so you are unable to afford him.

● It is the keeping of a horse that is the really expensive bit, not the actual buying. While you are paying out to keep someone else's horse it is often not feasible to save for your own or enough lessons to keep your riding up to scratch.

The big advantage of having a horse on loan is that it gives you an opportunity to discover what horse owning is really like before you make a massive financial commitment. Try to loan a horse during the winter as well as summer - it is lovely riding out on a warm evening, but it is a much fairer test of your horsy devotion to drag yourself out of a warm bed during the freezing winter months, battle with cold, rain and mud, move endless piles of soiled bedding, dry out soaking rugs and get down to the real nitty-gritty of horses all for barely an hour's riding, snatched hastily before work!

Useful addresses

British Horse Society, British Equestrian Centre, Stoneleigh, Kenilworth, Warwickshire, CV8 2LR

Association of British Riding Schools, Old Brewery Yard, Penzance, Cornwall, TR18 2SL

British Show Jumping Association, address as for BHS

Equine Behaviour Study Circle, Grove Cottage, Brinkley, Newmarket, Suffolk, CB8 0SF

Farriers Registration Council, PO Box 49, East of England Showground, Peterborough, Cambs, PE2 0GU

Pony Clubs and Riding Clubs, same address as BHS

Riding for the Disabled Association, Avenue R, National Agricultural Centre, Kenilworth, Warks

Scottish Trekking and Riding Association, Tomnagairn Farm, Trochry, By Dunkeld, Perthshire

Points of the horse

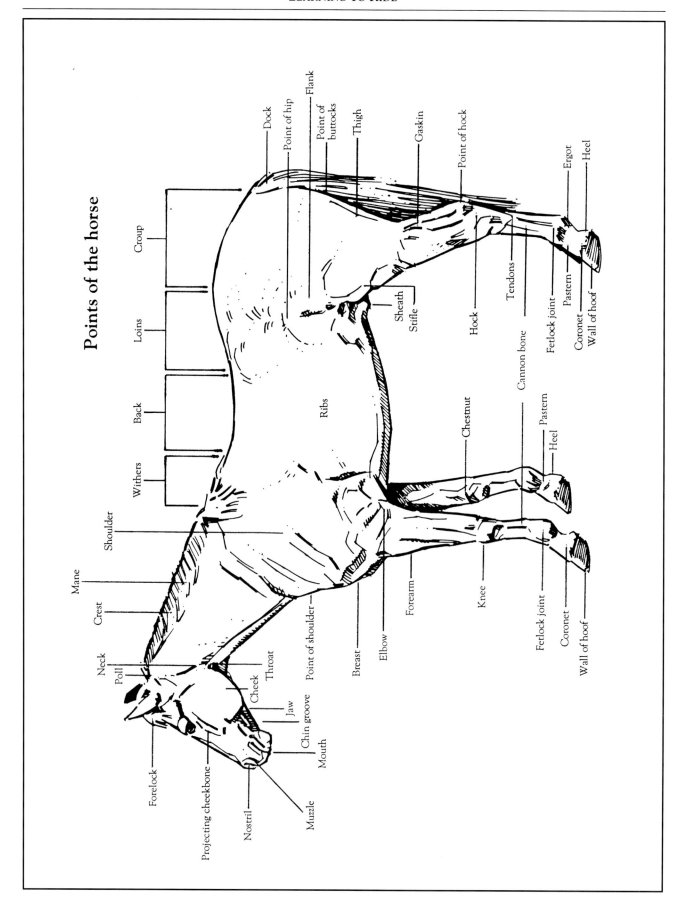

Dock
Point of hip
Point of buttocks
Flank
Thigh
Gaskin
Point of hock
Ergot
Heel
Croup
Loins
Back
Withers
Sheath
Stifle
Hock
Tendons
Fetlock joint
Pastern
Coronet
Wall of hoof
Ribs
Chestnut
Cannon bone
Pastern
Heel
Shoulder
Mane
Crest
Neck
Poll
Point of shoulder
Breast
Elbow
Forearm
Knee
Fetlock joint
Coronet
Wall of hoof
Throat
Cheek
Jaw
Chin groove
Mouth
Forelock
Projecting cheekbone
Nostril
Muzzle

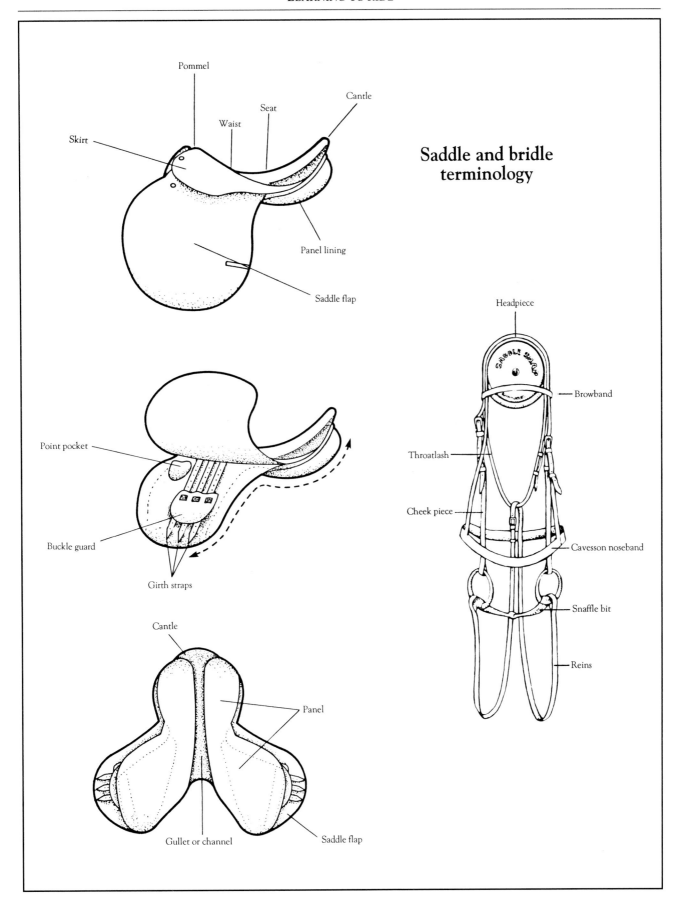

Pommel

Cantle

Seat

Waist

Skirt

Saddle and bridle terminology

Panel lining

Saddle flap

Point pocket

Buckle guard

Girth straps

Cantle

Panel

Gullet or channel

Saddle flap

Headpiece

Browband

Throatlash

Cheek piece

Cavesson noseband

Snaffle bit

Reins

A self-assessment test

Here's a fun exercise to see how you're doing so far! Just look at the photos in terms of the accompanying question, then check you answer with those given at the foot of the opposite page.

A. These riders are moving fairly quickly across open terrain. Comment on their positions.

B. How would you interpret this horse's body language?

Above C. Can you suggest an item of tack that might be a beneficial addition here?

Above right D. What comments would you make about this horse's bridle?

Right E. Comment on this rider's jumping position.

How did you do?

A. The first rider has quite a nice balanced and secure position. The second rider, however, has tipped rather too far forward, her knees are not so secure and her heels have crept up, with the whole of her lower leg position being rather insecure. If her horse were to peck she would be more likely to fall off.

B. The ears back, head thrusting, snaky neck, swishing tail and purposeful walk are saying 'clear off'. (In this instance the horse was seeing off another horse.)

C. A martingale would help as this horse throws her head up, making it difficult for the rider to exert control. The horse is being rather nappy and is using her strength against the rider's aids.

D. The cavesson noseband is fitted over the cheekpieces instead of underneath them and the browband is hanging rather low. There is probably enough room at the throatlash although it is difficult to tell on this picture.

E. The rider has a nice flat back, has folded well and has kept a good contact. However, you can see how her left heel has come up and the whole of this left leg position is not particularly secure. The position of the heel and left leg would indicate that the rider's weight is not centrally balanced - you can also see how her head is turned to the right.

PART 2

OWNING A HORSE

One of the joys of owning a horse, a close relationship with a trusting animal. But no potential owner should fail to be aware of the problems as well as the pleasures.

INTRODUCTION

WHY ON *earth do you want to buy a horse?* Advice to potential horse owners always seems to emphasise the untold joy and advantages to be gained when acquiring your own horse.

Not my advice!

Horse ownership can certainly be a wonderful way of life, but it *is* a way of life, and should not be entered into lightly. A cautious and pessimistic tone always enters my voice when I am asked to look out for a horse for a client, as I am all too often aware that it may be a project best left unexplored. However marvellous the creature may be, it is still capable of bringing emotional and financial misery to its owner and immediate family and friends.

It is most unpopular to point out all the drawbacks to horse ownership rather than the advantages, but a starry-eyed approach will almost certainly end in tears! I mean to tell you exactly what you may be letting yourself in for.

Horses are expensive time-absorbers!

Although it is not possible to give up-to-date costings on all the equipment required, you may find far more items of necessity to go with your horse than you first realised, and it will be sensible to add up all the foreseeable expenses before embarking on such a venture. It would be the utmost folly to buy a horse only to discover afterwards that the maintenance was too high.

Even if the horse is financially viable, are you genuinely prepared for the commitment of time and energy required to ensure that the horse is cared for adequately? Let's find out. . .

Carol Mailer

If you decide to take the plunge and buy a horse of your own, this is just a small section of the gear you will need.

1

WHY ON EARTH DO YOU WANT TO BUY A HORSE?

YOU MUST have some idea that horse owning might not be quite as straightforward as buying a car or motorbike, or you would not have acquired this book. So allow me to point out some of the drawbacks as well as any advantages; then at least if you *do* go ahead and buy a horse, you cannot say that you were not properly prepared!

● *It has always been my ambition to one day possess my own horse.*

If this is the case, nothing anyone can tell you will put you off once you are, or think you are, in a position to be able to afford this bottomless pit of expenditure. Not to mention the strained or ruined relationships with family and friends. Or the anti-social aspects of early mornings, late nights, dirty smelly clothes and constant penury. . .

● *I feel that the benefits of everyday riding will improve my health.*

Exercise can generally be beneficial to a person's wellbeing, but horseriding can also be classified as an extremely dangerous pastime or sport.

The British Horse Society estimates that at least one serious accident occurs every day, and as they often involve motor vehicles, death and serious injury is not uncommon, both to horse and rider.

Even if you avoid falls or serious accidents, your health may still suffer if the horse kicks you, treads on your foot, squashes you against the side of the stable, or bites you with real malice. Very painful bruising and nail damage will certainly be the result of the horse treading on your toe with a sharp jumping stud in his shoe, so do not be too complacent about the healthy aspect of owning a horse. You will almost certainly see the inside of your doctor's waiting room

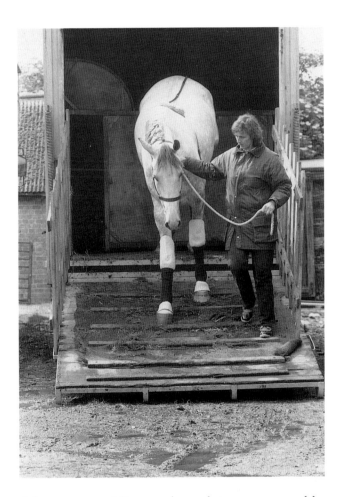

A dream come true! Your own horse - but are you prepared for all that goes with it?

more frequently once there is an equine member of the family to cater for.

Allergies can be a real nuisance, developing suddenly after exposure to hay or straw or shavings, or even an allergy related to the horse itself. Desensitising procedures may be uncomfortable and tedious and are not infallible, so the only solutions to this problem are to put up with it or avoid the

Left Healthy exercise, but this girl is in imminent danger of being trodden on and sustaining rope burns on her ungloved hands. A strong pony like this can do you damage even when you are only on the ground.

Below left The responsibility and expense of keeping the horse comfortable will rest with you. Riding is the glamorous part of horse ownership - much of the day-to-day care is very routine.

offending contact. If that turns out to be the horse, you really do have a big problem.

● **I am fed up with lashing out money on riding lessons and hacks.**

Maybe you think that buying and keeping a horse will be far cheaper than having lessons twice a week at your local riding centre. It is perhaps costing you £20 to £30 a week to enjoy yourself, and it would be very comforting to think that for that sort of money you could have a horse at your disposal for 24 hours a day. Please do not kid yourself!

The riding school proprietor has to pay for food, bedding, shoeing, shelter, labour, rates, insurance, vet and saddlery to enable you to pass the time of day on his horse. If the horse belongs to you, then so does the responsibility of all these other details.

The initial outlay to buy the animal, however pricey it is, is a drop in the ocean in comparison to the expenses that will immediately begin. Economy can hardly be classified as a valid reason for achieving ownership of such an expensive piece of goods.

● **I long for the companionship and affection that only a horse can bring.**

There are no negative aspects to this reason for wanting to purchase a horse, as long as you can afford to indulge yourself. But a puppy or a kitten would be cheaper and easier to manage as a pet, and just as affectionate. There would be no need for much outlay on living conditions either, or food and shoeing, not to mention insurance.

Still, if you have made up your mind that it has got to be a horse or nothing, you are probably too far gone to dissuade!

● **Circumstances have combined to provide me with the opportunity of achieving my heart's desire in becoming a horse owner.**

Perhaps you have moved out of town and into the country where there is a field or stable with your new home, or the possibility of accessible horsy accommodation in the neighbourhood.

There are bound to be more opportunities to keep

An obviously happy pair who have forged a real partnership with each other.

a horse in the country than in a built-up area, and it will certainly be more economical. If you do move to a property with paddocks and stabling, it would seem to be a shame to leave them uninhabited.

Also you might feel that a horse would serve the same purpose as a lawnmower and keep the place tidy. Remember that a goat or sheep would do the job twice as well and at a tiny percentage of the expense. A donkey would be cheaper to buy and maintain than a horse or pony, and would be just as loving. It might not be quite as much fun to ride, but it would certainly keep the paddocks down. Or you could rent the field and stables out to some horse-mad people to use for their animals.

However, if you really are keen to own your own horse, then what better circumstances exist than having it under your own care and supervision for 24 hours a day. The sheer luxury of constant access needs to be experienced to be believed, but do remember that other members of the family may not be aware of this.

You should point out to them at length all the

This home-kept filly is quite content. Note the sensible railed fencing and childproof lock.

advantages of a home horse against the expense and inconvenience of an away horse. If they are not horse inclined this might be difficult, so emphasise the economy of it all. That sort of logic usually works best.

● **To be honest, I feel that owning a horse is a status symbol, the thing to do in my particular social circle and financial circumstances.**

Acquiring a horse changes so much of the lifestyle of

its owner that it would be most unwise to enter into ownership unless you have thought the whole thing through properly.

Many cases of neglect have been caused by owners not understanding the commitment necessary to keep a horse, rather than lack of funds available for the enterprise. Please try to be honest about this.

If all you want to do is appear on the hunting field or in the show ring because it is 'the thing to do', consider hiring a horse for the occasion instead of buying one. It will serve your purpose just as well, and at the end of the day you need feel no responsibility to the animal other than returning it safely to its owner.

A superb hunter, the type that would quickly find a new home if you decided to pass him on.

There need be no stigma attached to appearing out on a hireling, if people know that you are well able to afford your own horse but are not bothering to do so; pressure of work is always a good and often genuine reason for remaining horseless.

If you decide that you still want to own the animal but are disinclined to want it as a family member, keep it in the best livery you can find so that its material needs are catered for without being any trouble to you other than in a financial capacity.

Then you can be assured of a decent horse available to you at a moment's notice without wondering if last week's hireling is fit and ready for another outing, or has been booked by someone else.

If you find that equestrian activities are not all you expected them to be, the nicer the horse you have bought, the easier it should be to sell it on. So do try

to find the right sort of animal in the beginning, not one that may be a liability if it has to go.

It will certainly be difficult to admit to yourself that you may only want a horse to be a 'poser', but it is best for all concerned, particularly the horse, if you have this understanding before you commit yourself to horse ownership.

● *I have discovered a horse I feel sorry for and want to rescue it.*

Why not leave the rescue jobs to charities that are fully aware of all they are taking on when they acquire an animal, whatever the source? A donation to their coffers would be far less torment and aggravation in the long run.

Everyone has heard of the wonderful horses and ponies that have been rescued from cruel and neglectful backgrounds, and how amazingly well these rescue jobs have turned out. But scant publicity has been given to the horses that can never be rehabilitated, who remain distrustful and dangerous for ever, and would be better off dead than continuing in

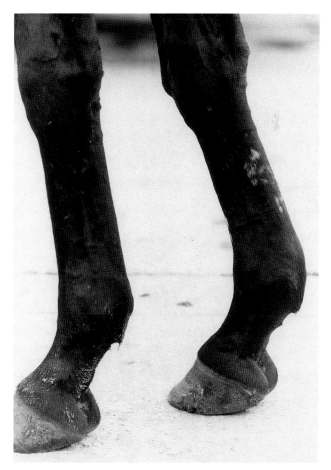

A horse with legs as bad as this would be better left to a charity to rescue.

mental, if not physical, torment.

If you are a kind-hearted person, brace yourself to stay away from horse sales so you will not be tempted to rescue a horse or pony better left to a professional organisation to save. If, however, you see a horse locally that is being neglected or ill-treated, report the situation to the RSPCA or local welfare body so the matter can be dealt with.

Having said that, if the heart rules the head and your pocket is adequate, then no advice is going to encourage you to leave things alone. You must just hope that your story will be one that has a happy ending and not turn into a tragedy, both for you and the horse.

● *My partner or child owns a horse already and I feel left out*

Perhaps you feel that a shared interest is a good thing, and in most activities it is, but horses sometimes bring out the worst in partners with jealousy

The whole family can enjoy being out and about with their horse, without owning animals individually.

causing all sorts of friction. If your partner is competitively minded and you are not, then there is a very wide area in which you will disagree.

A person who looks forward to a tranquil hack through the countryside in peace and quiet, enjoying the companionship of a like-minded animal, is unlikely to be on the same wavelength as a showjumping or polo fiend.

Unless you are extremely keen to do your own thing with a horse, why not consider the advantages of being a companion groom and helping out at shows and competitions? This does not mean being a general dogsbody. You will be able to enjoy the company of your partner's horse with none of the accompanying hassle that can go with it. A supportive role can be rewarding in any relationship and will enable you to spend whole days relaxing (?) together in the fresh air.

You will probably spend more time with the horse than the rider as they will be off course-walking, planning tactics and preparing themselves for the events ahead. All will go more smoothly if you are standing by to cope with all the little irritants that bedevil a competitor.

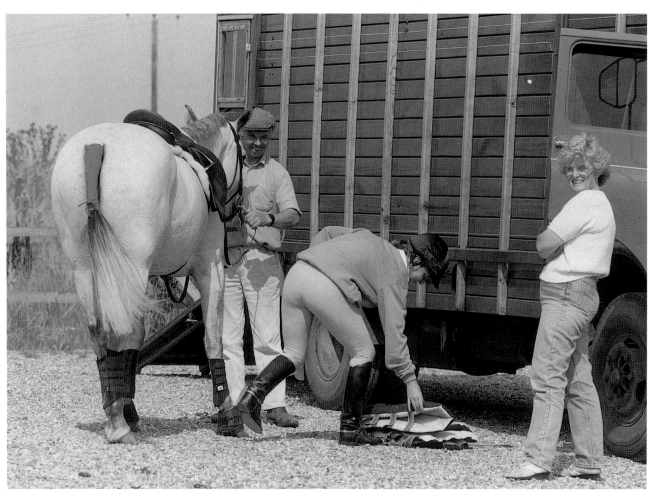

The crucial point can come when the supporter feels that he or she could probably perform much better and with far less fuss and attendance than the rider. In that case, if the partnership can run to it, the supporter will want a horse as well.

Enjoying a hack together in the country - but beware that more than one horse in the family can cause friction and jealousy.

It is quite distressing to seem to always give a negative view to the project of horse owning, but the prospective purchaser should recognise human frailty for what it is and not rush in impulsively without thinking things through thoroughly.

However, once you are set on buying a horse, you need help and advice on how to go about it, as you certainly do not want to end up with a costly mistake on your hands.

2
BE PREPARED

THE FIRST thing to sort out before you even look at a horse is where you are going to keep it, and if you are lucky enough to live in a horsy area there should be many options available to you.

Horses at home

Unless you are buying a native breed, you will certainly need to have shelter from the elements for the

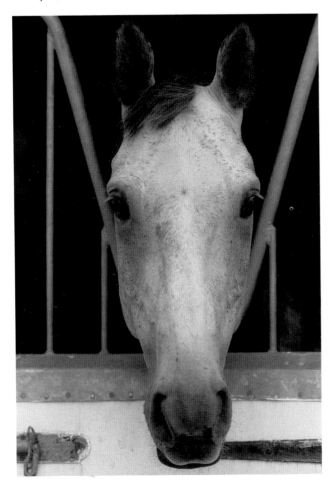

animal. Even many hardy native types enjoy their home comforts, and will not take kindly to being out in all weathers, particularly the heat.

If your garden or paddock is very small, half an acre or less, this need not be a deterrent if the horse can be properly exercised for at least an hour and a half every day without fail. Many horses seem to prefer only a couple of hours of freedom in the paddock to do their own thing before returning to the security of four stable walls and a comfortable bed. As long as they are able to look out and be nosey, this seems to keep them happy.

Beware of letting them get bored, as this all too often leads to stable vices like boxwalking and 'weaving' (shifting weight from one leg to the other and moving head and neck from side to side).

An ideal set-up at home for one horse would be a stable, hay, feed and bedding storage, and a small paddock of at least an acre divided into two or three areas.

A tack room can now be considered as an open invitation to thieves, so you would be wiser to keep expensive items of saddlery in the house rather than

Before considering the pros and cons of keeping the horse yourself, are you completely satisfied that your knowledge and experience is adequate for all the tasks involved? Pony Club and Riding Club tests have evolved to encourage members to show that they have attained certain standards of horsemastership. Even if you do not wish to belong to any organisation, the test requirements will show you what standard you should achieve before taking sole responsibility for a horse. Contact the British Horse Society (tel 0203 696697) for information.

Even a horse who 'weaves' is happy if he can look out.

110

Have you the time and inclination to keep the fields free from droppings, and the stables mucked out?

outside, and put up with the inconvenience of carting them back and forth to the horse.

Advantages of horses at home

● The horse is close at hand to be loved and supervised by the owner.

● There are no travelling expenses and time is not wasted going to and from the field or yard.

● You can make and change your stable routine without upsetting anyone else.

● Your horse is accessible to you 24 hours a day whenever you wish to see it, and your routine need not be interfered with by other people.

● It is *cheaper* than having to pay out for livery somewhere else.

● It is more satisfying to assume full responsibility for your own horse rather than relying on other people to do things for you.

- If anything disastrous happens you will know where to allocate the blame.

Disadvantages of horses at home

- You may not have time to see to the horse every day.

- You may not want to do all the messy chores involved with keeping horses, like mucking out, grooming and carting hay and feed about.

- If you are at work all day the horse will be left unsupervised.

- If you go away, special arrangements will have to be made for looking after the horse.

- The horse will lack companionship if it is kept on its own, and to keep a pony as a friend will be expensive and time-consuming. Horses are naturally very gregarious and prefer to live with equine company, so you may find an 'only' horse turning sour and miserable.

- Your lifestyle may not allow for the routine care and attention that a horse requires.

- If you are a first-time owner, you may lack the necessary experience and knowledge to enable your horse to exist safely and comfortably.

- Maintenance of grassland to keep the field fit to graze will need farming tackle, so if you want to keep the paddock in good order you will either have to hire a local farmer to do this or an agricultural contractor. Both will prove to be expensive.

- You will have to buy in and store all the feed that your horse will need, and bulk buying for one horse only does not work. The feed may go off before you use it.

- You will have to find a civilised way of disposing of the muck. Market gardens or farms may be persuaded to take this commodity off your hands, but do not imagine that they will pay you much for it, however superior the quality of the straw and the horse.

Shavings or paper bedding are unacceptable in horticulture, so you will have to get rid of that alone and unaided. Skips are an option, but this will prove expensive and inconvenient, so you may have to resort to dustbin bags and the local tip.

Soiled paper bedding may have to be bagged up and taken to the local tip.

Renting a field and/or stable

With the farming community in the doldrums this is a very real option. In the not too distant past, many farmers had a distinctly anti-horse attitude, but dwindling profits and Government 'set-aside' schemes have encouraged farmers to make way for the horse as an extra source of income.

Advantages of renting

- You will still have control over your own horse and be able to set your own routine.

- Your horse may well benefit from companionship as he will be unlikely to be the only horse in residence.

- If you are a first-time owner then there may be someone on site with possibly more knowledge than yourself if you are in need of help or advice.

- The farmer will have an interest in keeping the grass and hedges or fencing in good order.

- Depending on the sort of landlord you get,

you may find that he is willing to sell you most of the food and bedding your horse will need. If he does not make hay or keep livestock feed himself he will certainly know a man who does.

● Disposal of the muck should be no problem in agriculture, although you will be hard put to persuade the farmer that bits of the *News of the World* blowing round his fields are acceptable. Shavings are slightly better, but you should be prepared for the farmer to stipulate that only straw bedding can be used. If your horse suffers from an allergy you may have to take it elsewhere.

● Stables in older farms are often beautifully built from brick in an old-fashioned yard setting and infinitely superior to the prefabricated wooden ones offered on sale today. They are cooler in the summer and cosier in the winter if they have been properly maintained, and are

Well-maintained fencing is essential, and grass needs to be harrowed regularly to keep it sweet. If you are lucky, maybe the farmer from whom you are renting will look after this side of things.

less susceptible to all the damage done by an average horse.

• Security in a farmyard may be better than you could arrange in your own home. As the tackle and equipment used on modern farms is so expensive, farmers tend to take more security precautions than in the past, so if your horse lives next door to a combine harvester, he may well be protected by the farmer's own security network, usually alarms or lighting or, even better, guard dogs.

• If other people keep horses on the farm you may be able to arrange for them to look after your horse if you go away or get held up at work (on a reciprocal basis, of course).

Disadvantages of renting

• You do not actually own the land or stable and will be subject to any restrictions the owner may impose after your original agreement, unless this agreement is legally binding. You are almost certain to find that horse letting will be on a casual basis as farmers and landowners will not want to create formal tenancies in case this may be detrimental to them in the case of future development possibilities.

• Unless your horse has a paddock to itself, there is a strong chance that it may be bullied or bully other horses itself, both circumstances leading to kicking matches and subsequent injuries.

• Bad advice can be offered to an unsuspecting owner, either through ignorance or malice, by people sharing the facilities.

• Many farmers are barbed wire fans and see no wrong in using it to fence horse paddocks. Even a sensible horse is susceptible to the most horrendous injuries caused by entanglement with barbed wire.

• If the quality of the fodder and bedding that the owner has on offer is not good enough for you, he may take offence if you shop elsewhere.

• Bedding may be restricted to material that the owner can dispose of easily.

• Beware of dilapidated fixtures, unsafe doors and protruding nails. Do not forget that it is possible that the stables have been used to store all manner of sprays or poisons, so they must be thoroughly cleaned before horses use them again.

• Because the owner is all too aware of theft and vandalism on his property, the security measures may be restrictive for your access to your horse. Although this certainly has its good points, you may feel that your horse is left too long without a visit because the place is locked up or the guard dog is out.

• Although it's great to have other horse-minded people about, they may not get on well with you and advice or help offered may turn into interference.

Full livery

This is a super luxury way for an owner to keep a horse. The yard should be responsible for virtually everything that the horse and owner require. Mucking out, feeding, tack cleaning, grooming, shoeing arrangements, worming schedules and possible transport will be available, but it will be at a price. This is certainly the most expensive way to keep a horse, but can be satisfactory if the yard has a good reputation and continues to earn it.

Advantages of full livery

• The only thing you should have to worry about is paying the bills.

• The yard should have more 'clout' with the local services such as farrier, vet, and feed merchant than an individual owner.

• Your horse should be well looked after and have company.

• In full livery, your horse should be exercised if you wish, and even schooled if you stipulate it.

• There will be no problems if you are held up at work or want to go on holiday.

• The yard should have facilities such as a manège or indoor school, and may also have jumps or cross-country schooling fences.

• If you are a novice owner, you will be able to seek help and advice from the yard supervisor, and will be able to find similarly minded friends with the other horse owners in the yard.

• There is far less chance of your horse suffering an undetected illness or lameness where the yard is responsible for the animal's welfare. In a good yard, if anything is wrong with a horse the supervisor will call the vet first, then the owner.

Above Look for a livery yard that keeps its muck heap as tidy as this. The standard of the rest of the yard will thus also be high.

Below Arrangements can be made for your horse to be schooled, but you must be prepared to pay extra.

Is the school well maintained?

This may be occasionally irritating, but at least it shows that the yard's priority is for the welfare of its charges.

● If the horse you buy is unsuitable, you will have a better chance of relocating it if you are in a yard, as the yard owner will be in touch with more people over a wider area than an individual horse-owner.

● There will be far less disruption on the domestic scene if the horse is kept away from home, unless the financial aspect interferes.

● The yard should be prepared cheerfully to do extra jobs like plaiting and clipping, and preparing horses for shows, although this will be at extra cost.

Disadvantages of full livery

● It is expensive. A decent yard is going to charge at least £70 a week for all-in livery, and inflation will push this higher in the future. Do not lose sight of the fact that keeping a horse is a luxury, and not to be classed as an essential.

● You may find that you lose touch with the horse and it will become fonder of the people who attend its needs and spend more time with it, particularly if you need to have it ridden or schooled for you.

● Schooling facilities may be available but not included in the livery charge. Find out exactly what you are getting for your money at the beginning so you do not get a shock when you get your bill.

● You need to make sure that your horse is maintained in the best physical condition suited to its work, so you must keep an eye on him when he is under someone else's care. If you were doing the feeds yourself it would be easy to check, so try to be around at feeding time occasionally to see that he is being given the agreed rations.

● Many livery yards give the owners free access to their horses, but sometimes this will be impossible for security reasons.

● The agreed use of facilities may be subject to alterations at short notice.

● If you are easy-going, your horse may not be as well cared for as the horse of an unpleasant or obnoxious owner. It is just a fact of life, but be on guard so that your horse is as well treated as the next.

● Travelling to and from the yard may prove time-consuming and add to the expense.

● Other owners and also the yard's supervisor may interfere a little too much for your liking. You could get the impression that you are only good for paying the bills and they would rather you stayed away more often. You may lose sight of why you bought a horse in the first place.

Above right A livery yard that is kept as nicely as this will not be cheap!

Right Check if the use of jumps and cross-country course will be charged extra.

Part livery

Part livery is exactly what it sounds like. The yard may agree to muck out and do early morning feeds and arrange to turn horses in or out, but that is generally as far as it goes. There is usually a supervisor/ groom/owner about to keep an eye on things, so if you are pushed they may do extra jobs for you, but it will be at extra cost.

Advantages of part livery

- It is cheaper than full livery.

- You will have more to do with your own horse as part livery will probably not include grooming and exercising, although this may be arranged if and when necessary, at extra cost.

- You should be able to establish more of your own routine, rather than fitting in with other horses' needs.

- If you are responsible for feeding, you will know exactly what your horse receives.

In part livery, the owner of the yard will have to dispose of the muck, so he may stipulate what sort of bedding you can use.

- Although you will be doing more for the horse yourself, there will still be people around the yard to go to for help and advice.

Disadvantages of part livery

- If you are short of time or away, you will have to expect to pay more for your livery charge if you still want the horse to be exercised and groomed.

- Travelling to and from the yard is just as expensive in time and cost, whatever sort of livery you have arranged.

- You will really need to go to the yard two or three times a day to check on the horse unless you can arrange for someone else to do it for you. This will all add to the expense unless you do it on a reciprocal basis with one of the other owners.

- If you do not conform to the yard's ideas on horsekeeping you may find a disapproving atmosphere surrounding you and your horse.

- You may be restricted to the type of bedding you use to enable the yard to be able to dispose of the muck satisfactorily.

DIY livery

Again, this is exactly what it says. Generally the owner of the yard will supply stabling and the use of a paddock, and everything else you will have to do yourself.

Advantages of DIY livery

● You will be in charge of your horse's welfare, feed, shoeing, veterinary requirements, and exercise schedule. Because it is a DIY livery there will be little or no interference.

● You will be more independent about where you obtain your food and bedding supplies.

● There should still be other owners in the yard if you need help or advice.

● You should be able to make your own routine, subject to any security arrangements stipulated by the owner.

● Most DIY yards will have feed and bedding available to purchase.

Are your muscles up to coping with a wheelbarrow on to this trailer?

● It should be easy to avoid interference from other people by varying your routine.

Disadvantages of DIY livery

● If you are ill or working, it might be difficult to get someone else to see to your horse.

● Again, the question of travel inconvenience.

● Most DIY yards use shared paddocks and this could prove difficult if your horse is inclined to get involved in fights. It can also be a problem catching your animal if everyone else's horses are still out.

● There will not be so much supervision in the yard and security arrangements will be slacker if different owners come and go at all hours.

● Although it will be nice to look after the horse completely by yourself, there will be little or no back-up provided by the yard which must occasionally prove inconvenient.

Other owners may not keep their gear as tidy as yours, and will constantly 'borrow' items, forgetting to return them to the proper place. Eventually, this will enrage you and an 'atmosphere' will be created.

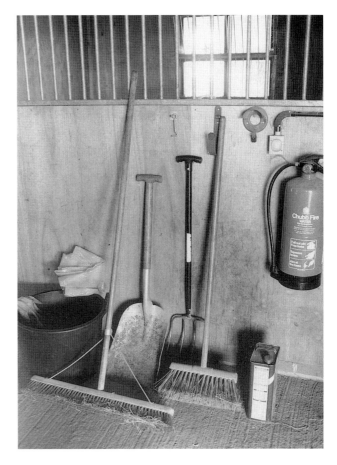

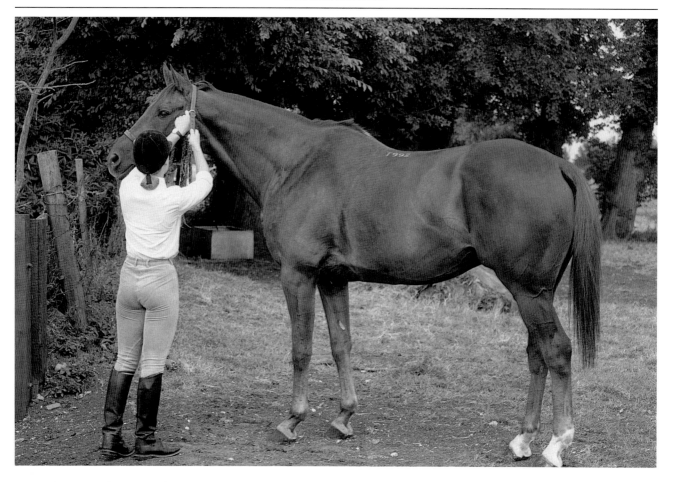

In DIY livery you have to fetch and turn out your horse yourself, so must pay attention to all aspects of safety. This is the correct way to turn a horse out - face him towards the gate before taking the headcollar off.

One of the maddening disadvantages of DIY livery is to see your horse disappearing with its companion when you want to ride.

Working livery

This type of livery is usually associated with riding schools and can be extremely beneficial to all concerned. The riding school proprietor will agree to keep the horse but will sometimes use it in the school; if he is honest, the horse will be used according to the prior agreement, and not over-worked, but some riding schools may not be so conscientious. The owner needs to have it absolutely clear before entering such an agreement exactly how long and often the horse will be working in the school, and what services will be offered in return. Everything should be agreed on before the horse enters the yard, especially responsibility for shoeing, vet and insurance. Grooming and tack cleaning should also be decided, as well as the price to be paid for this type of livery, as it will obviously depend on how much work the horse will be expected to do in the school.

Advantages of working livery

● It should be cheaper than other forms of livery.

● Your horse should be kept really fit and well for you as this will also be in the interests of the school.

● There should be more facilities available than at a smaller yard.

● Your horse will be exercised if you are unable to get there or are away on holiday.

● There will be plenty of company, both for you and your horse, and lessons will be easier to arrange when your horse is on site.

● A riding school is likely to keep longer opening hours than a private livery yard, so there will be greater accessibility to your horse.

● There will be no problems in finding a farrier, vet or feed merchant, but do make sure that your horse is well covered by insurance.

Disadvantages of working livery

● Other people will be riding your horse and may not be as considerate as you are, both with the horse and your tack.

● You will not be able to exercise your horse whenever you choose, as this may interfere with its school duties. Have this sorted out before the horse even enters the yard, to avoid misunderstanding. There are few things more infuriating than arriving to ride your own horse and discovering that it is already in the school under someone else.

● However professional the yard is, you will need to be vigilant and check that your horse is not being asked to exceed its agreed school work. Check, too, that it is being fed correctly and has enough bulk as well as protein to keep it fit and well. Also keep an eye on the tack and grooming, just in case your horse and its gear are not being well maintained.

● It will be difficult to stipulate that you do not want certain people to use your horse, so you must be resigned to putting up with it.

● If the riding school is busy, it may be difficult to find the place free when you can use the jumps or other facilities. It is possible that you might not get the same treatment as clients who may be paying more, so again get the agreement right at the beginning so it is quite clear what you are entitled to for your money.

● If the riding school closes for one day a week you may find that, whatever your preference, you cannot ride on that particular day.

There are many options of livery to discover, and only the more common sorts have been described. You could make joint arrangements with friends, caring for each other's horses on a turn about basis, and there are certainly many variations on this theme.

Wherever you decide to keep the horse, remember that the wellbeing and safety of the animal is of paramount importance, and all animals will respond best to a regular routine.

3
EXPENDITURE AND COMMITMENT

ONCE THE location of the horse's new home has been decided, there are certain financial commitments to be made before the horse even arrives.

Whatever type of animal you are buying, this expenditure will be pretty much the same, unless the animal is to be kept in full livery.

Pre-horse expenditure

1 Muck fork, pitch fork, heavy duty rubber gloves, skip or plastic laundry basket, shovel and rake
All these items should be available from either your local saddler, garden centre or agricultural supply store.

2 Wheelbarrow, muck barrow, hand cart or garden trailer and polythene rubbish bags for dirty bedding
Again, these should be found in the same stores. If you do have difficulty in finding what you want, check the ads in the horse press. Many firms will operate a mail order catalogue, especially useful for larger items.

3 Food and water buckets, hay nets, hay racks, mangers, tie rings and saddle and bridle racks or holders
Plastic dustbins are the most economical storage bins for food and can be bought quite cheaply from your local DIY store.

If you experience any difficulty in obtaining these things, try a catalogue from a stable manufacturer. Although their main aim is to supply actual stables, most of the leading firms supply, and are happy to sell, the fittings that go with them.

If you are going to be independent of livery, you may find it necessary to purchase and erect your own stabling. Check what planning restrictions apply in your area at the local planning office before you make a firm order.

4 Stabling
Most reputable stabling firms will submit the necessary planning application on your behalf, and can save you a lot of worry and expense. Prices usually quoted include 'supply and erection'.

The place to find the ads is in the classified pages of the horse press, but make sure that you send for the brochures of as many firms as you can find. Each firm's quality and service needs to be carefully compared; basically you will get what you pay for, and cheaper stables can generally mean they will not be so durable.

It really depends to some extent on what sort of horse you are planning to keep. A well-behaved 15-hands animal will need less room and will be unlikely to cause as much damage to its surroundings as an ill-disciplined 17-hands beast.

5 Baseworks
Any prefabricated stabling needs to stand on a concrete base and this will have to be completed before the chosen stables are delivered. You will have to obtain quotes for it from local building firms unless the stable manufacturer can recommend a contractor who is proficient and comparable in price to the locals.

You may feel that you can save expense and do

it yourself, but laying concrete is extremely hard work and if the specifications are wrong when the stables are delivered the firm will be unable to keep to schedule in putting them up.

6 Fencing

Again, send for brochures and obtain quotes if you need to put up paddock fencing. Most firms advertise their prices either supplied, or supplied and erected. Fencing is also very hard work, particularly the sort of substantial fencing required to prevent half a ton of horse straying, so think carefully before you decide to undertake this.

It may be most economical to buy the fencing and hire a local firm or farmer to construct it. Try the local plant hire firm to see if they have post-hole-digging aids to hire out by the day or week, but you do need to be fairly tough and practical to do it yourself. Barbed wire should not be considered as an option.

Muck barrows come in all shapes and sizes, but here is a luxury way of moving it. Note the cheap plastic netting to prevent litter blowing about.

Keep the food fresh with plastic bins, much lighter than galvanised metal.

Above far left A hanging manger is okay for some horses, but you will often find it thrown off the door when empty.

Left A corner manger is better as it can be removed to be cleaned when necessary. Note the string securing it to the bracket to keep it in place.

Above near left A suspended water bucket keeps the water free from bedding.

Above Schooling as well as grazing is safer when you are surrounded by solid post-and-rail fencing.

Long-term costs

That seems to cover most of the pre-horse expenses, so when the horse finally arrives, what will it cost you then?

1 Insurance
This is advisable as soon as the horse belongs to you and before it arrives on your property. It is a case of shopping around and getting quotes - many household insurance companies will also be able to arrange cover for the horse.

If you do not want the expense of full insurance, usually carrying a premium of around 10 per cent of the horse's insured value, it really is only common sense to arrange third party cover; this is also available with BHS membership. Obviously a fully comprehensive policy would be best, particularly if you stop to consider loss-of-use clauses and veterinary fees. Even the most innocuous injury or illness can run up a fortune in vet's bills.

2 Saddle, bridle, head collar, boots, bandages, rugs and any other gear the horse is used to.
If it is the first horse that you have owned, you will have to supply the animal with all its clothes without having any benefit of trading in unsuitable equipment.

Try to arrange storage to allow you to bulk buy hay. The merchant or farmer will then usually deliver and stack it for you.

3 First aid kits
Kits both for you and the horse should be kept in the tack room. You will be able to buy these already assembled from either the vet, chemist or local saddler.

4 Hay
Bulk buying of hay and bedding, especially at harvest time, is more economical, but will depend on your storage facilities. Over a year it would be sensible to allow 120 bales of hay if the horse is going to be living in, and obviously less in proportion to the time it may spend out at grass.

Even if the horse lives out all the time, it will still need some hay in the winter months to keep it in good condition. If you live close by to a decent supplier, it will be easier to buy the hay a few bales at a time, but keep a close eye on the quality as the hay is unlikely to come from a single source.

If at all possible, try not to feed new season's hay before Christmas. Slightly older hay is far better for the horse's digestion.

Quality hay will:
   a) smell sweet, not musty
   b) look greenish inside the bale, not yellow, brown, black or, even worse, mouldy
   c) have an even texture, not full of weeds or coarse grasses
   d) separate easily into flakes, not stick in great wodges
   e) not be too heavy in bales. Be suspicious of bales that weigh more than around half a hundredweight. They have probably got wet, and will be deteriorating inside.

5 Bedding
Straw is still comparatively cheap by comparison with shavings or paper bedding. Wheat straw is the best straw to use for horses as it is relatively coarse and not too palatable. Barley straw and oat straw are softer and make a very comfortable bed, but horses do tend to eat it more readily. It is very frustrating to carefully plan your horse's diet, only to have him preferring to eat straw instead.

Above Good-quality hay will fall apart into manageable flakes.

Right Paper bedding is an excellent alternative to shavings or straw.

More and more horses seem to develop a straw allergy and have to use other litter, so shop around for shavings or paper. You may live near a saw mill and be able to clear up the wood shavings very cheaply.

6 Hard feed

There should be animal supply stores within range to supply your bran, cubes, oats, coarse mix and minerals. The saddler sometimes stock a range of feed, and it can occasionally be purchased from supermarket-style 'cash and carries'. If you are only feeding one horse, do not buy in too great a quantity as the feed will go off before you use it up.

7 'Haylage'

Some horses are unable to eat hay without causing an allergic cough, and there are prepacked types of 'haylage' available. This is specially processed hay which is cooked or extruded and compacted into

Trailer or lorry? The choice and range of prices for both new and second-hand examples is huge.

polythene bales to eliminate allergy problems in the horse's diet. It will be necessary to buy a special net with smaller holes to use for this to prevent the horse gulping it down too quickly, but it will not take up so much room in storage.

8 Transport
Presumably the new horse will need to be transported home, and although you may plan a quiet life with little in the way of outings, transport costs need to be considered for essential journeys.

If you have bought a competition horse, you will certainly require transport of your own both for economy and convenience.

Hiring a trailer is the simplest method in the beginning, but only if you have a vehicle suitable for towing, and fitted with a tow-bar.

Horse boxes can also be hired on a daily or weekly basis, and if you do not know where to obtain one and draw a blank in the Yellow Pages,

go to a show. You will often see a trailer or lorry there with a 'FOR HIRE' sign on it plus a telephone number.

If you decide to buy, a decent second-hand trailer will cost you about £1,000-plus, and a lorry starting at around a little more for a very basic older model.

A super-luxury new horse box can set you back as much as a house, so again shop around the various showrooms until you find a year and model you can afford. Keep in mind that if you buy a trailer, there will be little maintenance costs by comparison with a lorry, no road tax to pay, and lighter insurance bills. However, there are far fewer accidents on the road involving lorries, and incidents with trailers are frequently in the news.

If you share a vehicle with friends or offer lifts in your own transport, it would be most unwise to travel without checking that your insurance covers both animals and not just the one that you own.

Family, friends and work

Deciding what the horse is going to cost you in financial terms is the easy part - you will soon know if you are able to afford the conditions and equipment the animal requires. It is not so easy to decide exactly what the horse is going to cost you in terms of family, friendship and work commitments.

Time
Unless the horse is kept in full livery, you will spend more time looking after it than riding. Horses need checking at least twice a day - once only is really not enough. Imagine if the horse were to injure itself just

after you have left it - it could be as long as $23^3/_4$ hours in trouble before being detected.

This may be looking on the black side of things, but horses have an amazing knack of getting into bother, however many precautions you may take. If you cannot spare the time to go twice a day, try to arrange for someone close by, or at the same yard, to keep an eye on it, and to ring you if there is any problem. You may be able to help out in the same way and check other owners' horses when they are unable to attend.

Wherever you keep your horse, make sure that you can be contacted in case of any trouble, and that the livery yard, farmer or whoever knows if you are going to be unavailable.

Some sort of arrangement should be made so that the people who are keeping an eye on your horse will feel free to contact a vet or blacksmith in the event of them being unable to get in touch with you. Your family, unless they are keen horse-lovers, may resent this intrusion on your home life, especially if you have previously spent all your spare time on call to them.

Work

Work has an annoying habit of interfering with the pleasures of horse-owning, but is a necessary evil when it comes to paying the bills! When you have to leave your work number in case of an equine emergency, ensure that you do not leave it with someone inclined to panic at the slightest little thing. A vet may need to be called, and sometimes very quickly, but many ailments can wait until after working hours. Flexi-hours or shiftwork are a tremendous boon to a horse owner as you can arrange to be in attendance to a vet or farrier during their normal working day. If this is impossible, you must expect to pay more for calling them out in the evenings or at weekends.

Most vets are happy to call without the owner being there, and to contact you later to discuss the problem or treatment. Farriers are usually happy to do the same, as long as the horse is well behaved, but you may find that you get a better service if you make sure the payment is left. Horse owners have been known to run up bills, so obviously prompt paying clients are preferable to more laggardly ones.

Personal relationships

Jealousy is not uncommon in the average household, and it is difficult for the non-horse-lover to understand his or her partner's or parent's commitment to the quadruped interloper.

Certainly your domestic arrangements are going to have a direct relation to the time spent with your horse, so you must try to ease the horse's routine unobtrusively into your lives.

Of course, difficulties will not arise if other members of the household are horse-mad and are prepared to be enthusiastic about the new addition. Even if they have previously shown no interest, you might be pleasantly surprised to find co-operation instead of problems.

If you have the right sort of relationships at home, the rest of your family will be only too pleased that you have achieved your ambition to become a horse owner. Even if the feeling at home is guarded neutrality, there should be little problem as long as you keep your equine routine in the correct perspective as far as the other members of the family are concerned.

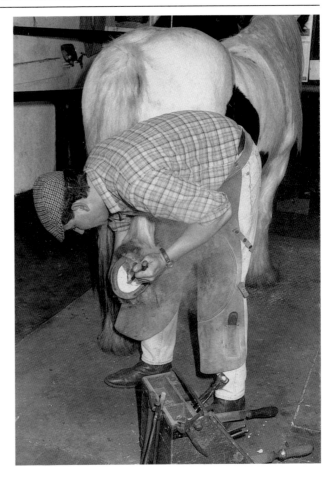

The farrier may be quite happy to shoe a well-behaved horse without you being in attendance. This does not mean, however, that you should expect him to catch a muddy animal and clean its legs before he can start his work. Make sure his job is as easy as possible!

The main difficulties will arise if you are not quite at peace with other family members, and there could be some resentment about the money spent and the time taken up by your new acquisition. It is almost guaranteed that at some stage you will need support from your family, so even if there is no enthusiasm, try not to alienate their feelings towards the horse.

In times of illness or pressure of work you will have to rely on someone else to help out with visiting, if not actual physical work, and life will be far easier if your family are there to turn to rather than outsiders.

Coping with an unsympathetic household

If you are the only member of the household interested in things equine:

• Refrain from being a bore. Even the most tolerant human beings get fed up with a one-sided one-topic conversation.

To help keep the peace and allay anxieties at home, do not get involved in equine activities that are more dangerous than you are competent for. Make sure you are as competent as this combination before attempting anything as hazardous as cross-country riding, for example.

• If you are the cook, serve the meals up on time. Being held up at the stables will not be accepted as a reasonable excuse by a hungry family.

• If you normally do the housework, try to keep to your everyday routine as far as possible, and if you take a few short cuts, do not let them be obvious to the rest of your household. It will be most unpopular if you try to enforce a new method of participation in the chores on an unwilling family, and the horse will get the blame.

• Do stick to a prescribed budget for the horse expenses, and do your utmost not to exceed it. Money problems cause a great deal of unhappiness in any relationship and you do not want your horse or your family to suffer because you have not done your sums properly.

• Ask for horse-related presents for Christmas and birthdays. As well as being useful, this will show that your interest is going to be serious and long-lived.

• Do encourage a disinterested partner to develop his or her own hobbies. It will only make an unpleasant atmosphere if you insist on a reluctant partner hanging around the stables when they would far rather be somewhere else.

• Resist the urge to get involved in equine activities that are more dangerous than you are competent for. The sympathy at home will be tempered by annoyance if you are crocked up doing something you were unwise to attempt in the first place.

• Be truthful about the expenditure. If you rely on your partner for financial help, it would be silly to disguise where the money is going. If you are independent in money matters, do not exclude them from the knowledge of how much everything is costing. Their disapproval may help you to keep your expenses at a manageable level.

• Encourage any enthusiasm for the horse with reservation. If you have only one horse in the family, you do not want the other members trying to take it over, but the time will surely come when it will be necessary for them to help you out. Ensure that they are sufficiently instructed in your routine to be able to cope if you are laid up, but be careful not to set the standard of management too high. Accept the fact that as long as it is fed and cleaned out or turned out, it will have to wait for you to resume control to restore the little luxuries missing during the temporary custodianship.

All the problems encountered with a disinterested family can be overcome if you are sensible, and you do not let it affect the comfort of their lifestyle.

Coping with an enthusiastic household

Enthusiasm for the horse on the part of the rest of the family is easier to deal with, but it is also not without its problems:

- You will be told what to do.

- Your social life apart from the horse will deteriorate.

- You will probably have to share the horse.

- Other members of the family may achieve better results on your animal than you do yourself.

- There will certainly be interference in your stable routine, and you will find yourself doing most of the jobs with little of the rewards.

- If another horse is required, it will double the expenses and time involved.

- If another horse is acquired, who will spend more time looking after it? Obviously the more experienced member of the family.

- One or other partner could be more ambitious in their riding aims than the other, which might lead to conflicting viewpoints on the use and treatment of the horses.

On the other hand, enthusiasm can have its advantages:

- Your family will be far more understanding of the time and expense involved with horsekeeping.

- You will be able to turn to them for help and be reassured that the help should be competent.

- The heavier jobs like muck carting or unloading hay may be delegated to stronger members of the family.

- All your leisure time will be spent at the same place enjoying similar activities.

- You will be able to bore each other.

- There will be no spare time available for other activities.

- If all the spare time is spent at the stables, you can ask for and expect some help around the home, and flexibility over meals and home comforts.

All the drawbacks of buying a horse should by this stage be apparent, so now you need to know how to go about it (if you still want to!).

4
FINDING A HORSE

LEARNING to ride not only provides you with the activity itself, but also the opportunity to meet and socialise with people sharing the same interests; it also may be the starting point in your quest to find a suitable animal. So let's look at the advantages and disadvantages of various places to search for your horse, supported by some cautionary tales.

The riding school

This could well be the best place to start looking, as the instructor there will be familiar with your capabilities as a rider. If there is a horse at the school you would like to buy, ask. The proprietor might be willing to oblige, particularly if you were to keep it on at the yard as a semi-working livery.

Advantages of buying from a riding school

• You will already be familiar with the horse you wish to buy, so you will not need to try it out - you know its capabilities.

• You will also know the owner fairly well, so there is no likelihood of you being 'done' by a stranger.

• The riding school will also know you and the horse well, and should be prepared to carry on with lessons if necessary.

• Presumably the riding school is in your neighbourhood, so you will not need to travel all round the country to view the horse.

• The riding school is a professional yard and should be able to provide any advice and back-up service after the sale, although you will justifiably have to be prepared to pay for it. This sort of arrangement has a distinct advantage over buying from a private individual, who may not want to know about any future problems encountered.

Disadvantages of buying from a riding school

• The horse will be used to being ridden by novices and may be unlikely to improve as you do yourself. As you gain more experience, you could find yourself wishing that you had been a little more ambitious in your choice of mount. It depends on your aims for the future.

• A riding school horse will have many companions and could resent the loss of his friends.

• If you live in close proximity to the school, the horse may nap back to its old stables, not because you are keeping it badly, but out of habit.

• The horse may be unable to settle in a new yard, however much attention it receives, especially if it now becomes an only horse.

• The horse could be difficult to ride out on its own if it has always been used to going out in a group.

Riding school night-mare
A very well-known riding school and livery yard had an exceptionally fine mare in the stables. She was an absolute saint to ride in the show ring, jumping or out hunting. She was so exceptional that about twice a year the owner was prevailed upon by a besotted rider to sell her. He always sold her, and for a goodly sum, and she always came back.

Once she was away from her own yard, she turned into a vicious beast, biting, kicking, bucking, rearing, and generally behaving in a totally alien manner to the horse with which the purchaser was familiar. Faced with this unmanageable savage, the new owner would beg the proprietor to take the creature back, as it was impossible to try to sell her on to someone else. Nobody was able to get near her to put a saddle on, let alone try her out.

There was little the new owner could say in defence of his treatment of the mare, as he had insisted on buying her because she was so perfect. It was obviously his fault that the mare turned on him, so he just wanted to get shot of her as soon as possible.

After much deliberation and 'horse-trading' talk, the original owner would let himself be persuaded to take her back, at an extremely beneficial discount on the original price. It is said that one of the new owners actually paid him to come and take her away as she was smashing up the stable yard! Surely an exaggeration. . .

Nobody knew this would happen the first time the mare was sold, and the original owner was as surprised as the new one that the mare could behave so badly. But once she established a pattern of this behaviour, the profit made on selling her expensively and buying her back cheaply more than paid for her keep over the years.

Eventually her reputation became more widely known and the opportunities to sell her became less frequent, but well into her teens she would occasionally leave home for a few days, only to return in triumph.

She always behaved impeccably at home and had obviously made her mind up that she would not settle in anywhere else. So don't get yourself lumbered with something like this. It could prove to be very expensive - and not in the long run, either.

Friend's recommendation

Once you are familiar with the horsy scene in your area, you will find that it can be possible to buy a horse on a friend's sayso, particularly if they have been involved with horses for a longer time than you. They will have a wider knowledge of the area and the horses that could be available for sale. You may even be able to buy a horse from a friend directly, although this could end up putting your friendship in jeopardy.

Advantages of buying on a friend's recommendation

● Hopefully, your friend will be acting with your best interests at heart, and will only recommend a genuine animal.

● The horse will probably live in the vicinity, so travelling and transport should be easier and more economical.

● A fair trial will be easier to arrange if your friend can act as mediator, and recommend you to the vendor as well as the other way round.

● Advice and help with the horse should be more readily offered if the friend has been involved in the sale, as they will feel partly responsible for the way things turn out.

● If you have not met the vendors before, they may become new friends and look forward to keeping an interest in the horse if it remains in the locality.

Disadvantages of buying on a friend's recommendation

● The friend could be biased, and only friendly in order to help sell a horse.

● You might not want to buy a local horse that everybody knows.

● The price for the horse will be well known and gossiped about locally, and there will be much speculation about whether or not you paid the asking price.

● Even if only initially, the horse may not go as well for you as it did for the previous rider, and you might feel that you are being compared unfavourably.

● Your friend might feel that a present is in order for helping you find a horse. Not too friendly, but it happens!

● However helpful the previous owners mean to be, it could easily get to the point of interfering with your routine and plans for the future of your horse.

Costly introduction
A lady hunting enthusiast had been looking for a horse for the coming season, and had approached many people in her hunting circle without success. Finally, someone with whom she was fairly friendly told her of a cracking hunter to be found in the next village. She thanked him for his interest, duly inspected the horse and bought it.

At no time was there any mention of the go-between having any financial involvement with the purchaser, although it did cross her mind that the vendor might well have slipped the gentleman a good 'drink' for producing a suitable client for the horse, a well-known practise in the horse-dealing world.

Imagine the lady's surprise when she received a bill from the friend for 10 per cent of the purchase price as an

Above left If your friend has recommended a horse, take her with you to view it. And if the owner chooses to ride in wellies, make sure you do not emulate her!

Left Your friend could be biased, and only friendly in order to help sell the horse. Make sure she is biased towards *you*.

Above A genuine friend will give an honest opinion.

introduction fee. Plus VAT! The lady was not amused, tore up the bill and returned it to the friend. She never did pay it, quite justifiably, but it was the end of a civil friendship, with both parties feeling aggrieved, and caused quite a lot of gossip and ill-feeling in their immediate circle of acquaintances.

If a friend offers to involve themselves in helping to find you a horse, clarify the position before they have expended any time and effort. However well you think you know them, you do not want to discover an unexpected financial commitment after the deal has gone through.

Advertisements in the press

All the horsy magazines carry a Classified Ads section, so you should have no difficulty in locating a vast array of horses available for sale.

Local papers usually also have a Horses and Saddlery section and will probably be the first place to look if you are limited for travelling time. A local horse will be far more convenient to view and vet, but obviously you will not have such a wide selection of animals to browse through.

Advantages of buying through press advertisements

• They will provide a nationwide selection of animals to be viewed, and also a fresh selection will be advertised every week or month.

• By comparing prices on paper, you will get a rough idea of values of different sorts of horses, which will give you an idea of the price you must expect to pay for the animal you desire. Most prices are inflated to allow for offers or haggling, so do not be too dismayed if everything that sounds nice is beyond your price range; allow for a price reduction of around 10 per cent on the asking price and you will probably be closer to what the vendor is actually prepared to accept. Occasionally you may find a real bargain if circumstances conspire in your favour, as in the accompanying instance. If the advert reads 'No offers' and you like the sound of the horse, wait a week or so and ring then. If the horse has not been sold, the vendor may be a little more amenable to 'talk'.

• The Trades Descriptions Act should protect you if you buy a horse through an advertisement which can be proved to make a false claim about the horse. This can be extremely difficult to invoke, however, so do ensure that any claims made about the horse and its ability can be verified before you put the money down.

• It will be very exciting to read through the ads, sorting out the horses that sound ideal, and fixing up to view, and you will find yourself really looking forward to discovering a fresh batch of horses, particularly if the previous week's scrutinising has come to nothing.

Bargain price

A nice horse was ambitiously advertised for around £5,000, resulting in a very limited response. Similar sounding horses on the same page were being offered at £3,000 'or near offer'. As it was not sold, the price dropped and dropped until it eventually changed hands for £1,500. It was still the same nice horse, but the circum-stances of the owner dictated that it be sold rapidly. The purchaser just happened to be in the right place at the right time, and had the nerve to make a substantially lower offer. If the owner had been sensible and advertised it at around £3,000, all the people originally put off by such a high price would at least have viewed it and possibly made a closer offer.

The horse was quickly sold on for £3,500, and turned out to be a very good animal, which, of course, the original owner knew all along. It is unusual to get such a bargain, and took a lot of nerve in waiting for the price to drop, but the purchaser had nothing to lose.

It is never sensible to put a silly value on your horse, however much you feel it should be worth, as readers will not bother to ring if apparently comparable animals are a couple of thousand pounds cheaper.

Disadvantages of buying through press advertisements

• There is one principal disadvantage in buying through a press advertisement, and that is becoming familiar with the terminology. A whole new interpretation of the English language can be discovered in the classified ads sections of the horsy magazines and you need to become conversant with this before you go tearing off round the countryside seeking unsuitable horses. Elucidation of some of the more common terms is given below.

Guide to terms used in classified advertisements

Good to box, clip, shoe and in traffic is a fairly standard phrase, but if any of those attributes are missing, you can bet there is a good reason why, and that they do not apply in this particular horse.

Blemish free is another phrase to invoke discussion. Exactly what would you consider a blemish? If you are buying a horse to show, the horse *must* be blemish free, having no lumps or bumps or scars. But if you want a horse with no *defects*, a few white hairs as a result of a cut or graze will not put you off and may add power to your bargaining.

Obviously it will be advisable to avoid a horse with massive scar tissue or enlarged hocks and knees, large curbs and active splints, but minor defects can be overlooked if they are not going to affect the action and performance of the prospective purchase. It is a fairly rare horse that reaches the age of seven or eight without incurring something or other that will show up as a slight mark or blemish.

A show jumper rang up about a horse advertised as a novice with great potential. It was exactly the sort of breeding that he preferred, and the horse sounded perfect in every way. It had a small amount of winnings under rules which could easily be checked, the size and weight sounded right for him, and he thought it would be ideal, certainly worth a look. The horse was a long way from home, and only as an afterthought, because the horse was advertised sound and ready to go on, the jumper asked if the horse had anything amiss with it. He explained that a veterinary surgeon specialising in legs kept a few horses in his yard, so the horse would be thoroughly vetted before purchase. There was a long silence at the other end of the phone, then 'Can't you get another vet?' No deal!

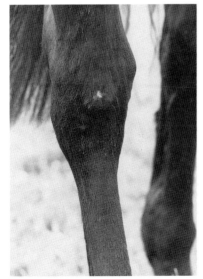

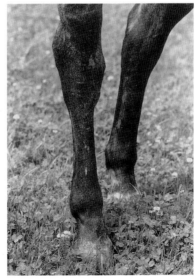

Above 'Good in traffic': if you need to ride out on the road, check that the horse is well behaved.

Far left 'Blemish free': although this scar will not cause any physical problems, the horse is definitely not 'blemish free' and is unsuitable for showing.

Left Avoid a horse with a hock like this. Even if it is sound at the moment, it will be unlikely to stay so.

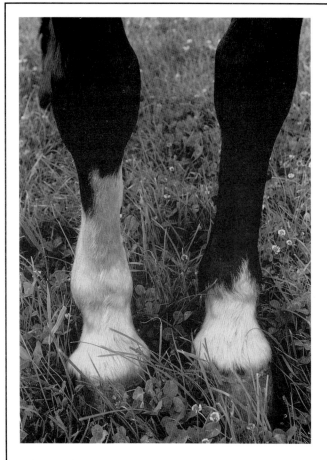

'Blemish free': an old hardened splint like this will not affect the horse's performance, but beware of a splint that is warm and gives the horse discomfort when pressed.

Any scar tissue or lumps will be pointed out during the vetting procedure, together with an opinion as to the future soundness of such a blemish.

Schoolmaster is another word that seems to be misconstrued in the context of horse ads. A 'schoolmaster' should be a trustworthy animal with no vices, it should be obedient and well behaved in whatever job it is supposed to specialise, and should be in no need of reschooling.

Genuine schoolmasters are very hard to find and, as you would expect, can command a good price as there should be a built-in safety factor with such an animal.

A genuine schoolmaster is not a flash horse, but a solid, workmanlike and pleasant-natured animal that will do exactly what is required of him, whoever is on his back, be it novice or experienced rider.

It does not have to be a 'slug', but it should definitely not be a tearaway. Putting the label 'schoolmaster' on an older animal just to sell it is not fair to the animal or the purchaser, and will only result in a deal which is unsatisfactory to everybody.

A livery yard sold one of its own ponies to a would-be client as a showjumping 'schoolmaster'. The client had little experience, paid a very high price, and expected to be able to go out to small shows and do well.

Unfortunately, the pony, which was a very experienced showjumper, did not take kindly to its new role in life. It did not want a novice on its back, and would take off in an alarming manner, often doing two circuits of the showground before the hapless rider could manage to pull it up. It had to go back.

The yard accused the rider of ruining the pony, and a miserable time was had by all. The pony was a genuine jumping pony, and because it was growing too elderly to cope with the bigger tracks, the owners had thought that it would be suitable to go back to smaller

'Schoolmaster': trays and water ditches are irrelevant to this little chap, and he is teaching his rider not to view them with apprehension. The only clue to his experience is the harsh bit in his mouth, and you must presume from this that he would be unmanageable in a snaffle. It is also most unlikely that he will be eligible to jump in novice classes.

'Schoolmaster': it should be a solid, workmanlike and pleasant-natured animal that will do exactly what is required of him, whoever is on his back, be it novice or experienced rider. Here a genuine example gives its young rider every confidence to tackle the water jump for the first time.

jumps with a novice rider. They just did not recognise the world of difference between a pony that tried to please its rider at whatever level, and a pony that resented a novice on its back, preventing it from doing its job in the way it chose.

The client, lacking experience, had seen the pony going really well and had thought that it would only be necessary to buy that animal to achieve a modicum of success.

Has been seen to weave or crib or windsuck or boxwalk. The implication in the phrase 'has been seen' is that the stable vice is not yet a positive habit and that the horse will not always do it. Rubbish!

If such a phrase has to be inserted in the ad you can rest assured that the habit is long-standing and is not going to be easily cured.

'Weaving' can to some extent be controlled by using anti-weave grilles, and crib-biting or windsucking by operation or using a special collar designed to stop the vice, but boxwalking is slightly different. You could either turn the horse out all the time or provide it with a companion like a sheep or goat.

In Scandinavia, where horses have to spend so much time inside because of the climate, the problem is alleviated by placing a rabbit in a cage in the corner of the stable. There are also many cases of dead sheep, goats or rabbits. However, it is easier to avoid the problem by not buying a horse with these hang-ups. Surely you will be able to find a horse without them somewhere.

There was a most attractive advert in one of the horse mags for a five-year-old German bred with dressage potential, and he certainly did not disappoint the prospective purchaser. He was a very expensive animal and she was determined to try him out thoroughly, so she went to his yard on three different occasions to ride him before she made up her mind.

She did not think it suspicious that someone was in the stable with him on every visit, and when he was vetted the vet did not remark on this until later revelations came to light. For as soon as the horse arrived at his

'Has been seen. . .': this horse's evil attitude to its neighbour may not have been discovered if the owner had been first on the scene before the arrival of the prospective purchaser.

new home, he proceeded to wear a groove in his stable floor. Not only did he boxwalk, but he paced out at double time, and it was certainly a long-standing habit.

The lady immediately rang the former owner to insist on the horse returning as he was obviously going to be unmanageable for her yard, and was told that the horse had never ever done it before.

While this was patently untrue, it turned into a very nasty situation, and the vet was required to certify to the horse's unsuitability.

Fortunately the cheque was stopped at the first sign of this problem, and eventually the original owner took the horse back.

He really had little choice as he was getting no money and the lady threatened to take an ad in the horse mag to state precisely what had happened to her and who she had bought the horse from.

So if you have any remote suspicion that things may not be as they seem, turn up to view the horse earlier than arranged, and try to get an unimpeded first look in the stable.

Keen ride is another description that is open to different interpretation. The horse might be enthusiastic about its work, or it could be completely loopy and unstoppable.

Suitable for beginner is always a comforting phrase to read if you are a novice rider, but check carefully on the age of the horse, particularly if it has not been mentioned in the ad. It is just possible that the horse is only suitable for a beginner because it is worn out.

Readvertised due to timewasters is often given as the reason for a repeat advert, but just who is wasting the time?

Arrangements were made over the phone for a lady to go to view a four-year-old gelding that was just 'backed' and supposed to be hacking quietly round the farm. The price had already been discussed and found acceptable, providing that the horse was as described. It was supposed to be blemish free, very quiet, and ready to be brought on by a competent rider.

When the lady arrived she found that everything was okay as far as the horse was concerned. She rode it round the farm and it behaved beautifully. It was a very nice animal and she was delighted to have found something to suit her, although it had taken a good deal of time and trouble to arrange the viewing, besides being almost at her limit price-wise.

The journey home took two hours, she contacted her vet straight away to arrange for him to inspect the horse, and rang the owner. No more than $2^1/2$ hours had elapsed since speaking to the owner, so she was absolutely staggered to hear that they had received another offer of £1,000 more for the horse. Of course, if she felt she could come up with another £1,000, the owners would much rather that she had the horse as she had got on so well with it! The lady indignantly declined, as much on principle as financial circumstances, and the sale fell through.

Two weeks later she was surprised to see the horse in the paper again under the emphasised heading 'Only Readvertised Due To Timewaster.'

Who was the timewaster? It was only a con trick to try to extract another £1,000 from the would-be buyer, and when the trick backfired, the owners had no alternative but to advertise the horse again and chose to brand the blameless buyer as a timewaster.

Horse-dealing really does seem to bring out the worst in some people, and their scruples disappear. Gazumping is certainly no way to sell a horse, but it is not always the fault of the vendor when the buyers are labelled as timewasters.

A Pony Club-type pony was advertised as being suitable for both novice and more experienced riders, and was duly viewed by a family with two daughters. They tried the pony on two different occasions, jumped it at home, hacked it out alone and rode it in company. The pony was well-mannered, good-looking and competent for most Pony Club competitions. As the family were looking for a replacement for a lame pony, they asked if they could take the pony to a rally the following week to see how it behaved out. Reluctantly the owners agreed, although they felt that the pony had already proved that it was reliable in every way.

The pony returned after a successful outing, having been placed in a small competition, and the owners were then informed that the pony was not quite of a high enough standard to get in the team.

There had never been any mention of this ambition to the owner, and the pony had never been stated to have such potential. It was being sold as an outgrown, nice Pony Club-type - the owners in no way misrepresented its ability, and it would have been ideal for any normal child.

Because the family had been dwelling on the pony for at least a week, the owners had put off anyone else viewing and lost several potentially more suitable clients. In the meantime, a new set of ads were in the mags and the chance to place the pony had to be deferred until it could be readvertised, 'Due to timewasters'.

Left 'Snaffle mouth': a lovely little Connemara cross horse going beautifully in a plain snaffle and cavesson noseband.

Below left Still a snaffle bridle, but a more severe type. The noseband also suggests that the horse is quite strong and needs a good rider rather than a novice.

Snaffle mouth should denote that the horse is controllable and happy in an ordinary snaffle bridle, but when you ring, check to see what sort of snaffle it is used to, and also what noseband is worn.

Careful detective work on the phone should save you money, time and travelling expenses, so before you pick up the receiver make a list of all the points you want to clarify.

Up to weight can also be misrepresented in the ads and needs some careful discussion on the phone.

A horse was advertised in the local press as being 'up to weight but very light on its feet with floating action'. This implied a free-moving middle to heavyweight horse with a decent action.

It was a carthorse! It had to be booted and kicked to get it out of a walk and its trot was very stilted. The client never achieved a canter as it was too much like hard work, yet the owners thought it was a wonderful creature with showing potential.

A petite lady scanned the ads for a lightweight hunter and eventually seemed to find the ideal sounding horse. She travelled 200 miles to see him, looked over the stable door, and travelled 200 miles home again. What had been described as '16 hands' was at least 16.3 and big with it, far too large for her. The owners were terribly apologetic for their mistake, and the rather lame excuse was that they hadn't measured him lately.

Discovering that the lady was rather small, they had minimised his size to her on the phone, saying he might be just a touch over 16 hands, but perfectly suitable for a lady. Perhaps he was, but not a small lady. Presumably they had hoped that because she had come a long way, she would at least try him, and possibly be

'Up to weight': this horse could truthfully be described as 'up to weight' as he could comfortably carry several stones more than his jockey weighs. He is certainly no slug!

Try to avoid the situation where you are confronted with a giant. This horse's 18 hands is a little too large for this rider.

won over by his (gargantuan) charms, even if he was a little on the large size.

There is not much more to be done in a situation like this unless you try even more stringent weeding out over the telephone. You can always pretend as much as the owners, and imply that you need a heavier or larger, or smaller or lighter, horse than you really do, and see if they adjust their sales pitch accordingly. It might save your petrol!

Well bred The absolute classic remark was made by an Irishman to a client who was very persistently questioning him about the breeding of his prospective purchase: 'Sure, and who would you like him to be by?'

It happens, so be on guard. It could just as easily be 'Sure, and how tall do you want him to be?', or 'Sure, and how heavy do you want him to be?' Don't forget, Irishmen do not have a monopoly on blarney! The Welsh, Scottish, English, and all the Continentals have more than a touch of it themselves when it comes to buying and selling horses.

Sadly outgrown is another expression to be found in the ads, and at least this one should be relatively easy to check - ask to see the previous rider. There may, after all, be a more sinister reason behind the horse's availability on the market, and at least you can be on your guard if you confirm that the ex-jockey was a midget.

Teenagers shoot up like weeds, and you will often be able to find a really nice horse of around 15 hands that is being wasted as it has been outgrown quite suddenly.

Never stops is a very sweeping statement and far from being a recommendation - it could imply that the horse is headstrong and rather stupid. Even Milton stops on the odd occasion when he knows it is wiser than going on, and nobody would describe him as dishonest.

Never sick or sorry is a curious phrase that is usually employed to describe an older animal. The implication is there that the horse will carry on regardless in its work, shrugging aside all adversity and staying super-fit year in and year out. However anyone could think that this would influence a prospective client is amazing. Everyone knows that flesh and blood will eventually succumb to illness or injury in some way or other, and the fact that it is healthy so far has no direct relation on its well-being in the future.

Obviously, you will choose to buy a strong and healthy looking animal as opposed to a sickly looking little weed, but there are no guarantees that either of them will remain trouble-free in the foreseeable future.

Totally unspoilt or **Untried** implies that the horse is very green but ready to begin its serious work. The suggestion is that the horse will be very good in the future and nothing has happened yet to upset him - but perhaps his early education has been minimal. Conversely, it could also mean that the horse has been completely unreceptive to any attempts to school him, so is being sold on as green when in fact he may be no good, or on the verge of developing problems that the owner has no wish to solve.

A buyer went to view a five-year-old threequarter-bred horse that was a really nice type and had been described as 'totally unspoilt'. He was very impressed with the animal until he went to get on it - the horse skittered away across the field, and was a job to catch.

The owners passed this off by saying that the horse was so green that they had only ever got on him in the yard, so the buyer duly used the mounting block and managed to get in the saddle.

The horse took off again across the paddock, bucking and fly-kicking, and dropped the would-be buyer, thankfully without causing any injury.

'Well,' he was told, 'you can see that he knows nothing, can't you?'

The horse had obviously been broken badly and was starting to develop all sorts of problems. The owners had not persisted in trying to correct him, resorting instead to describing him as unspoilt, purely to obtain a better price. Luckily the buyer was sensible enough to realise that this untried horse may have been tried a little too far, and left well alone. But a less experienced person might have believed all the sales talk and bought himself a bundle of trouble, fondly imagining that the horse only needed to learn kindly the correct way to behave.

Open to any vet seems to be straightforward enough, and on the surface is uncontroversial. Prospective buyers will obviously prefer to use their normal vet, as long as he will travel, since he is the one who is going to attend the horse in the future. Problems can arise if the same vet is used by both parties, as he might prefer not to be in the middle should the horse fail. Vendors might protest about the use of a particular vet if they have fallen out with him before, and it is not surprising that any vet failing a horse will, if only momentarily, be a most unpopular person.

Once the vetting has been arranged, all parties concerned are assured that the deal is serious, and the condition of the horse is the only thing preventing money changing hands. Some vets can be notoriously nosey, and the first question they ask is 'How much are you paying for the beast?'. If you want the vet's opinion on the horse's value, tell him. However, if you prefer to keep the price to yourself, do so! It should be totally irrelevant to the vetting procedure as all that should concern the vet is if the horse is sound or not on the day.

If the vet is not to be put off by your reticence in revealing the agreed sum, grit your teeth and tell him a lie, lowering the price, not raising it. So many vets pull a face if they think that their clients are spending too much on a horse, and they usually have their clients' best interests at heart, but by the time they are called in to do the vetting the price will already have been agreed. You certainly do not want someone implying that you

have been foolish to pay so much for the animal. It is none of their business if you want to squander too much of your hard-earned cash on a horse they think is not worth it.

You should also be wary if the vet tells you of a horse he knows that is either better or will not cost so much. If you do the asking, fine, as vets are looking at horses every day and can certainly tell you if they have seen something to suit you elsewhere - but you do not want the information to be volunteered. And neither will the vendor.

X-ray examination on more expensive purchases is now commonplace, with some vets advocating it automatically, not because there is a suspicion of lameness, but because they feel that they should try to foretell the future. Certainly X-rays should be used in diagnosing a current problem that has shown up in the vetting procedure, but may be considered irrelevant if the horse is sound.

A lady who had just lost a horse with navicular disease found a new horse that suited her perfectly. He passed the vetting with flying colours, until the vet, aware of her previous loss, suggested X-raying the feet just to make sure. The horse was then turned down as a result of its X-rays as it was felt that it showed enough signs on the X-ray to develop problems in the future. Seven years on, the horse is still fine.

Another horse was produced for vetting, X-rays were taken, and the horse pronounced A1 in every way. Eighteen months later it had to be put down due to navicular disease.

These may seem extreme cases, but although the importance of X-rays is obvious in diagnosing existing trouble, there is always a possibility of misinterpretation for a long-term view.

So 'open to any vet' is not always true. For example, the vendor may object for several reasons:

- The vet always fails his horses.

- He does not want the horse X-rayed.

- The vet has a lousy reputation.

- He does not want the vet knowing his business.

- He won't have the vet in the yard.

It is entirely possible to discount all these objections and insist on the vet of your choice, or the

Is the horse really 'open to any vet'? Better to make sure!

deal should be off. But do have some sympathy for the vendor in this matter - some vets are well known to have preferences for particular sorts of horses, and can also be well known for their dislikes. If the horse is dumped, the owner is the one who has to live with the knowledge that his horse *may* be faulty.

The only thing to insist on in a vetting if you are not 100 per cent trusting of the vendor is a blood test. Many vets nowadays do this as routine, particularly if the horse does not look quite right to them even though there is nothing to actually pinpoint as evidence of unsoundness. A blood test should show if the horse is on any drugs, particularly pain-masking ones, so if the vendor shies away from a vet because he knows this is going to happen, steer clear of the horse.

Sold through no fault of his own or **Reluctantly for sale** are real tear-jerkers, and unfortunately will be true in the vast majority of cases. Financial stress, loss of grazing or stabling, pregnancy and loss of interest will all be good reasons for the sale of a horse, however reluctantly, but you must not discount the fact that these reasons might not be genuine.

The horse might be sold because there is something wrong with it, and the owner is hoping to disguise this by claiming that circumstances are responsible. Occasionally dealers use this ploy, so try to check back copies of the magazine in which you saw the ad to see if the same phone number has previously applied to another horse claiming the same hard luck story.

In fact, if you are opposed to buying a horse from a dealing yard, do the same thing. If the same number appears regularly as a private-sounding ad, but with different horses advertised on each occasion, you can be fairly certain that it is a dealer rather than a private seller. You should ask yourself why he is possibly trying to disguise the fact that he often has horses for sale. Reputable dealers are quite happy to use their name and number without subterfuge, and their ads are generally larger and more expensive to insert than those of the private one-off advertiser.

To good home only is another phrase to be discounted. No owner likes to be thought of as uncaring in passing his horse on, and equally no prospective buyer would like to admit to providing a less than perfect home. Obviously, the vast majority of owners are very concerned about where their horse is going, but it is a fairly useless phrase to put in an ad.

Inspection of the new premises is far more practical, and should be mentioned by both sides on initial contact.

First to see will buy is a wild claim. How anyone can state that their animal will suit the first person to reply to the ad must either be supremely confident or more used to dealing in used cars. It is this sort of extravagance with words that makes one suspicious of everything to do with buying and selling horses.

Sure to go to the top is another claim that only a fool would take much notice of, particularly if not qualified by the usual addition 'in the right hands'. How anyone can confidently predict their horse's future in such a description defies belief.

A family went to view a horse that the owners confidently predicted would carry the 16-year-old daughter to the top in eventing. It was only 15.2 hands, its dressage was very good, and its jumping was supposedly up to a satisfactory standard; it certainly seemed to fulfil their expectations. It jumped very well in the school, particularly down a line of three fences, which the owners gradually increased to a good size.

The trainer of the daughter had gone with them, and asked to alter the distances slightly. This met with a bit of resistance as the distances were 'correct', so she compromised by removing the third jump. The little horse went down the line and still jumped the non-existent third fence. It was obviously extremely familiar with the grid, and had been well drilled over it.

Unfortunately the family were well out of their area and unable to arrange to try the horse somewhere away from home, where the jumps would be unfamiliar to it. However, because everything else was okay, because the owners assured them that it had won many prizes in the jumping and cross-country sphere, and because the owners claimed that they were really interested and expected to follow the daughter's success in the future, the horse was purchased.

When the horse proved to be very limited in its jumping ability, the former owners did not want to know. Any criticism to be levelled was levelled at the

daughter, who was a genuinely competent little jockey.

So the horse was sold on. A nice little horse indeed, but certainly not good enough to go to the top, and a bit more investigation might have revealed this. As the former owners were quite knowledgeable, it is more than likely that the horse was misrepresented as being far better than it was, but this would be very difficult to prove.

A horse is not going to the top in its own backyard, so however far you have to go, make sure that the horse proves its ability to you beyond any doubt.

Occasionally you can see **Capable of going to the top** or **Top-class potential**. This is a more acceptable description, and not so exaggerated, but still implies a bit of fortune telling.

An amateur showjumping lady rang up about a horse she had seen advertised as 'genuine top-class potential', but as the horse was still within her price range she was a bit suspicious.

The horse had not actually gone to a show to demonstrate its ability, but it was jumping 'a 5-foot pole at home'. She therefore decided that it was well worth looking at, particularly as the owner assured her that it would go Grade A in a very short while. All this confidence, remember, when the owner had not even seen the lady, let alone watch her ride.

The lady found a nice little horse that was fairly ordinary in appearance, but in no way looked as if it would go to the top. It did not have the eye-catching presence seen in most of the better sort of showjumpers. However, as she had been prepared to find a more ordinary type than an equine superstar, she was not too disappointed. As long as the horse could jump a bit, she felt it could be perfectly adequate for her modest ambitions. All she hoped for was to have fun, go round the smaller classes and not disgrace herself, and own a nice little horse that would not let her down at the level of competition she was happy in.

The horse was duly tacked up and the owner mounted to demonstrate it. Once he started to jump, the horse showed a distinct lack of enthusiasm, and obviously preferred to keep all four legs on the ground - he really did not want to know.

The lady was getting very fed up watching this sorry performance and asked when it was going to jump the 5-foot pole. The owner immediately brightened up, hopped off the horse, and shouted up to his house for assistance. Two girls came out with lunge whips, the owner untacked the horse, put up a 5-foot pole in the manège and the three of them proceeded to chase the horse round until it did actually pop the 5-foot pole.

The lady was speechless. The horse had still been reluctant, and only jumped because of the insistence of the lunging whips. It was obvious to anyone that he certainly would not choose to do so unaided, let alone with a rider on board.

The owner, oblivious to the aura of disapproval surrounding the lady, was very proud of himself and his horse. He really had it in his own mind that the horse was absolutely top class, and just needed bringing out to show its full potential.

When she told the owner what she thought of his animal and his training methods, he was amazed, disappointed, and then angry. 'Timewaster' was mentioned by both parties, and the lady departed horseless.

The horse was still being advertised six months later, although not in such glowing terms. Harsh reality must have eventually dawned on the owner and forced him to be more truthful about the horse's actual capabilities and not its imagined potential.

It is a common failing in ads for exaggeration to take the place of accurate description, but it is sensible to remember that owners can and do see their horses through rose-tinted glasses, and can honestly believe that their horse's virtues and capabilities are second to none.

Careful weeding out over the phone can sometimes prevent timewasting in this sort of situation, but not always, as the owner genuinely believes he is telling the truth. Even if the lady in this instance had asked a bit more about the horse's actual record, she might not have been deterred, as glossing over the fact of a 5-foot pole only when loose schooling would still have encouraged her to view.

Only when she arrived and saw for herself that it would not do, was she assured that it was not the right horse for her. It might, however, have been just the job, so when you are going viewing you will just have to be prepared for disappointment and accept it as part of the 'fun' of buying a horse. The really annoying thing about such an expedition is the knowledge that you might have missed something far more suitable while wasting time and effort on a no-hoper.

BSJA winnings £60. Jumping well in Newcomers This description sounds as if there has been no exaggeration, and on the surface seems to be self-explanatory. The British Show Jumping Association office is open for anyone to ring in and check the winnings on their computer (tel 0203 696516) so this cannot be in dispute.

However, wild tales have circulated over the years about horses that have 'gone round the clock', that is won enough prize money to put them in a higher grade, and then been re-registered as novices. It has happened occasionally, but is usually detected and the owners penalised. The only way you will know for sure that the horse is not one of these 'ringers' is to trace its history back through previous owners, which is not always an easy task.

Misrepresentation of the horse and its winnings is taken very seriously by the BSJA and they make every effort to ensure that it does not happen. Rumours are often started by unhappy members, usually if their horse has been beaten by a better one, and need not be taken seriously unless proof is produced.

In one area of the country there is a notorious chap who does not seem able to help himself. He has started no end of rumours about local horses being ex-Grade A, usually to explain why his own horse has not beaten them, and now no one who knows him takes him seriously. But someone who does not know him well could easily be taken in and make a frivolous objection or spoil somebody's sale. One day someone irate enough will sue him, but it has not happened yet, and he still keeps on.

The 'jumping well in Newcomers' part can also be checked up to a point. If the owners are a little cagey about what class the horse has won most of its money in, the BSJA computer will tell you. You would expect a horse claimed to go well in Newcomers to at least have some place money in this class, but if all its winnings have been in Discovery competitions, a lower-grade class, perhaps it is not up to doing much more. In 1992 the limit of winnings in Discovery classes was £150. Perhaps the horse is only for sale because it is getting near the limit of Discovery and is not good enough to go on and do well in Newcomers.

You cannot downgrade a horse once it has won money, so question the owners carefully and insist on details of what it has actually done in the next class it will have to go in. The same applies for horses getting to the top end of Grades B and C. They may only be for sale because they cannot cope with the bigger fences.

Other difficulties can arise through buying a horse that is advertised *accurately* by its winnings.

A lady had a problem after buying a showjumper already qualified for Newcomer and Foxhunter region-

'Jumping well in Newcomers': showing photos of a horse jumping well in competition is a good selling aid, but before you buy check with the BSJA exactly what the horse has done.

al finals, and its record at the BSJA checked out.

The horse had plenty of ability and was a real gentleman, and she thought she had got exactly the right horse to take her on. It was most unfortunate that she was not really up to starting off over this size of course and was horrified to arrive at her first show and be scared silly at the size she was going to have to tackle.

Of course, the horse had won too much money to go in smaller classes unless it was non-competitively, so she was stuck. A case of not looking before you leap!

Generally the ads with winnings displayed are most helpful, but just read between the lines to make sure the horse is really what you want.

Won and placed unaffiliated opens, hunter trials, R.C. teams etc are claims made frequently in the ads, and can also be checked out. But not so accurately.

There is no governing body for unaffiliated shows,

and the organisers rely on owners' consciences to keep them in the correct classes. Even when challenged about doubtful eligibility in a novice class, it is difficult to check if the owner has been forgetful about previous winnings or completely untruthful. The only sure way of knowing if a horse is ineligible is if the same judge has made a personal note of the animal's winnings on previous occasions.

If a horse has won an unaffiliated open, he will probably be out of several restricted novice classes, so try to pinpoint exactly how much the horse has won before you buy it. It will be very embarrassing to be challenged about eligibility once the animal belongs to you, and you really do not want to have to compete in classes bigger than you anticipated before you are ready.

If you are looking for a horse to do opens with, you do not want to find it incapable of jumping the bigger tracks, normally starting at 3 ft 3 in to 3 ft 6 in, so insist on seeing rosettes or some sort of record to support the ad claims.

Won and placed BHS Events or **Always jumps Double Clears** are frequent statements applied in the sale of event horses. The BHS (tel 0203 696697) monitors winnings for eventing and dressage horses based on a points system, so it is just as easy to contact them for the horse's record as it is for jumpers to speak to the BSJA.

Any claims about the horse's prowess can be checked, but you will still see the sort of ambiguities or implications applied to these horses as in the above phrases. The horse might have won something or other under rules, and this is not in dispute, but check whereabouts.

Some courses are ideal beginner tracks, and some novice courses are notoriously more difficult. Find out where the particular horse has done well so you know what sort of conditions it has won under. With the emphasis on jumping double clear rounds, it might mean that the horse's dressage is pretty grim, so check on the dressage scores as well. Even if a horse is doing double clears round intermediate tracks, it may never win a

thing or gain any points if its dressage is too horrendous.

Do not take the owner's word for it if it can be checked out. It is only a phone call and will help you to make up your mind with all the facts in front of you.

As you can see, finding a horse through press advertisements does have its drawbacks, and unless you develop the knack of weeding out untruths, you could waste a lot of time and money in your search.

If anything can be checked up independently, *check it*!

Below and above right 'Always jumps Double Clears': accurate showjumping and a bold approach to cross-country will give plenty of double clear rounds. . .

Below right . . .but perhaps the dressage is not quite as good.

Dealers

There are many horse dealers, ranging from the small dealer who sells maybe two or three horses a year to subsidise his business, to the vastly more commercial dealer with a large yard, numerous staff, and a heavy turnover in horses.

Advantages of buying through a dealer

• The dealer has a reputation to protect and will not lightly lose his good name to make a quick profit.

• The dealer will usually exchange an animal if the new owner finds it unsuitable after purchase, but not necessarily for the original price.

• There will usually be a selection of animals to see all in one place, so you will have a wider view of the market without the time and effort spent in travel.

• A dealer will often be able to find a horse to suit you, even if he does not have one immediately, and he will have infinitely more contacts to draw on.

• A dealer of necessity will have his own transport and will be able to arrange to deliver the horse for you if required.

• It is in the dealer's interests as well as your own that he should provide a satisfactory after sales service and be available to help practically or with advice about your new purchase.

• The dealer will not have an inflated idea of the horse's value. Obviously he is going to make as much profit as he can from the deal, but it will not be in his interests to gain the reputation for overpricing his animals. He would not get any clients!

• The dealer will probably be recommended to you by previously satisfied clients, so you will be able to see already if he is good at matching up horses and riders.

• There are no complications involved about why the horse is for sale. It is for sale because it is the owner's business to sell it, so you are not going to get a lot of sob stories or hard luck tales. If you do, you will be able to ignore them with a clear conscience.

• The trial facilities will probably be better than at a private yard, as the business will be geared up to show horses off as advantageously as possible.

• Many dealers offer inducements like a 14-day exchange warranty. Check any insurance liability before entering into such an agreement.

Disadvantages of buying through a dealer

• Horse dealers are often depicted as shady characters, rather in the same mould as second-hand car dealers, so you are bound to approach them with a certain amount of caution.

• You may get rather high-pressure sales talk. They are used to selling horses and will have the gift of the gab, so will recognise what pitch to make in your particular case.

• The prices might be higher than perhaps you were expecting to pay, but most dealers will talk (haggle) about a price and allow offers to be made, so naturally they are going to allow for this little foible of human nature in the original asking price.

• Animals that have been accepted in part exchange will be in the yard, so unless you are given a good reason why they were originally rejects, steer clear of them. However well-behaved the dealer has made them, they might revert to type when away from his experienced handling.

It is very easy for the dealer to give a valid reason for having some of his horses, and most people will find them acceptable. Finance, college, marriage, pregnancy, old age (the person, not the horse), outgrown - though do be wary about 'outgrown' being a good reason for parting with a 16.2-hands horse.

Double dealing?

A decent lady rider bought a working hunter horse that tried her patience in every way. Although very good looking, and quite capable of winning in decent company, he developed a nap. Every time he went into the ring, he hung towards the exit, eventually going so far as to rear and dance about in public.

She persisted with the horse because he had so much potential, but in the end she gave him best and decided to sell him on. Because she could not guarantee his behaviour, she contacted a professional dealing yard to take him so she could wash her hands of him entirely.

She was completely honest about his misbehaviour as well as his record of wins, and was prepared to, and did, take a substantial loss in the price she had originally paid.

The owner of the yard then proceeded to try and sell her another horse in part exchange that he had in the yard for reschooling as a worker. She graciously declined, and went away relieved that she had the sense not to buy a horse with maybe the same problems as the one she had just got rid of. Not surprisingly, the reschooling bit put her off, so she made a completely fresh start, with no financial entanglements to consider, even if considerably poorer in pocket.

Dealer's ploys

The most common phrase dear to a dealer's heart is 'I've got someone coming to look at it tomorrow'. Not only dealers use this phrase - it is well known in the private sector too, as well as in the used car lots.

The standard answer should be 'Fine - if you can sell it, do so, and good luck'. Do not be pushed into a corner by this sort of attitude if you cannot make up your mind. Far rather take the chance of losing the horse than being coerced into something that goes against all common sense. If you have to hesitate and cannot give a straight answer, it is probably not the right horse for you anyway.

Another phrase that springs to mind is 'It's the first time we've seen it do that'. This usually applies to some form or other of misbehaviour, like bucking, rearing, napping or running away.

It can mean that the reschooling has not been quite as successful as was first thought, and the horse needs a bit more time before it is ready to be viewed. Again, this is certainly not unique to dealers, as private vendors may also have a lot to answer for.

This sort of ploy is potentially far more damaging than trying to gee you up in making a decision. It can be downright dangerous.

'He's never done that before'

A lady rider travelled all the way from Yorkshire to Devon to view a five-year-old Hanoverian. After a long and expensive time on the phone, she decided that the horse was worth the trip, and duly arranged to turn up the following day.

When she arrived the horse was absolutely it! All she had been hoping to find and more. It behaved impeccably in the stable while she looked all round him. If there were any blemishes, she could not find them.

Mother and father were in attendance, but the owner, the daughter, who normally rode the horse, had been called away on urgent business. This should have set the alarm bells ringing as it had only been 12 hours before that the appointment had been fixed up.

However, the lady had not travelled all that way to be put off by a little thing like not being able to see it ridden first. Husband, grumbling all the way, had come with her, and was quite competent to tell her how well she looked on this beautiful horse.

The creature was an absolute dream to ride and she went round his paddock at walk, trot and canter - the best mover she had ever sat on. . .for 10 minutes.

Going past the gate for the fifth time, the horse decided that he had done enough. He stopped and reared. She was terrified. Rearing was the one vice she abhorred above all others, and although a capable rider, she never claimed to be the bravest of jockeys at the best of times.

When he had got all four feet on the ground again, father was quick to rush over to tell her she must have jagged the horse in the mouth as 'He's never done that before'. Because she liked the horse so much, she half believed him, and carried on for another circuit of the field.

Exactly the same thing happened at the gate again. He stopped and reared up, and instead of returning quickly to the ground again, he stayed up. She discovered that he was very accomplished at this performance, as he hopped across the field on his hind legs. All she could do was hang on round his neck and pray that he would not slip. Occasionally he would vary the performance with a leap and plunge, but always returned to this two-legged dance.

She shouted and kicked, and husband shouted too, but it was only when the horse decided he had done enough that the performance ended. All the owners would say was 'He's never done that before'.

This was so transparently untrue that tempers were quickly frayed, and much unpleasantness ensued. The buyers left for home, husband furious and wife dismayed. This was supposed to have been a private sale, and there was no hint of the Devon couple having any more horses, but as the wife still looked in the ads for a suitable horse, about every six weeks, the same phone number had a different horse advertised.

There are two lessons to be learned here. Go to a dealer who admits and is proud of his occupation, and never get on a stranger's horse until you have seen it ridden first.

A dealer may try to gazump the price. He will explain it by saying that he had incorrectly entered the horse in his books, and he could not possibly let it go at such a low price as he would be losing money. Doubtful!

VAT might crop up as an extra after the price has been settled, so do ensure that you know where you stand before your heart is set on a particular horse.

Any decent-sized dealer will have a large enough turnover to be VAT registered, and should already include it in the price quoted. You really do not want $17^1/_2$ per cent added to an already expensive purchase, unless, of course, you can claim it back yourself.

Dealers have acquired a somewhat shady reputation through the years, and most purchasers are rather cautious about buying horses from them. It has to be said that many dealers deserve the reputation of sharp practising, and you are advised to only approach a dealing yard if it has been recommended to you by someone you trust. Often the purchaser tries to outsmart the dealer, rather than walking away, and will probably come out of any deal badly in the long run.

Set-up

An extremely sharp businessman took up hunting, and knowing very little about horses in general, hired his animals for the day. He soon made acquaintances in the field, and as his riding prowess increased, he thought he ought to look for a couple of hunters of his own.

The yard from which he regularly hired his horses offered to help him find two suitable hunters, but the businessman rudely declined. It was a well-known hunting livery yard with a high reputation, and the owner would occasionally buy and sell. The businessman, assuming that the owner was that lowest form of life, a dealer, told him brusquely that he was quite capable of finding his own animal.

He looked at horses for weeks. It became an obsession to find two nice horses without the help of the owner of his normal hirelings. He was on the point of giving up when one day while out hunting he heard of a couple of nice hunters about 50 miles away.

Everyone in the field was well aware of his obsession and opinion of dealers, and he was told of these two horses with a little touch of malice by a friend of the owner of the livery yard.

'Mind you' he was assured, 'they aren't cheap. They're a private yard.'

The businessman was well up to paying an expensive price, and he did. The horses were just what he wanted, albeit very pricey, and he never stopped to consider that it was a rather large yardful of nice horses for one private owner to maintain.

The deal was done, the horses were bought, and placed in the hunting livery yard. The businessman never realised how he had been set up. He had bought nice horses for sure, but he had certainly paid through the nose for them. He would have had a far better deal if he had let the livery owner acquire the same horses for him through the 'trade' and not been so suspicious of the motives.

Instructor's recommendation

Although you do not already own a horse, you may have decided who you will get to help you when it is finally found. It is only a natural step to ask them to help you find one.

Advantages of buying on an instructor's recommendation

- Presumably the instructor already knows how well you ride, and will be able to assess your capabilities accurately to match you to a horse at the correct level.

- Through her other clients, an instructor will be more aware of a likely animal coming on to the market before it is advertised, and you might get first option on it.

- It will be in the instructor's own interests for you to find a nice horse on which to be taught.

- The instructor will probably be able to pinpoint more drawbacks or defects than an inexperienced purchaser.

Disadvantages of buying on an instructor's recommendation

- There is always the chance that the instructor has a financial interest in the deal, so define in whose interests they will be working.

- She may be in a hurry to find you a horse to increase her own revenue.

- She may not be quite so particular as if she was looking for one for herself.

- There could be delays in setting up a mutual viewing time when more people are involved.

Loans and adoption

A loan arrangement can work wonderfully well as long as both sides understand and accept their respective responsibilities.

Advantages of a loan arrangement

- There is no initial outlay in terms of a purchase price.

- It is an ideal temporary measure if you only need a horse for a short time, perhaps before going to college or similar circumstances.

- If the animal becomes outgrown or no longer required for any reason, it will be the owner's problem to relocate it.

Disadvantages of a loan arrangement

- The horse never actually belongs to you.

- You may feel the owner is too restrictive about the conditions of loan.

- It will always be an extra worry if anything goes wrong, however well insured you are, since you are not the only person involved.

- The owner will be able to repossess the animal on a whim, so you will be unable to make solid plans for the future.

Adoption

Adoption or loan of a horse from a rescue organisation can be immensely rewarding and the agreement that they draw up is well worth considering if you are lending or borrowing a horse. Some sort of contract along the same lines would save an awful lot of problems on both sides in any loan arrangement.

The Wood Green Animal Shelter located at Godmanchester in Cambridgeshire (tel 0480 830014) often has horses available for adoption, and sets out the accompanying conditions for loan.

Although this agreement seems terribly long-winded, on reflection a would-be borrower should be quite happy to sign. After all, it is only designed to safeguard the welfare of the horse involved, and that should also be a prime concern of the borrower.

A lender, also, should be quite happy with the terms set out. There may be some amendments in respect of matters for which the owner feels he would still like to take responsibility, either financially or otherwise, but the basic framework is sound and sensible to follow.

Conditions of loan

1 The keeper will not be a dealer in horses or other animals, nor an agent for such a dealer.

2 The horse will be kept as a pet and will not be used for vivisection, for experiments, for stage purposes or for breeding.

3 The keeper will regularly, at his own expense, feed, water and exercise the horse, keep it in good condition and health, properly care for it in a humane manner and keep it in a suitable environment.

4 Should the horse not be castrated, the keeper will at his own expense arrange for this operation to be carried out by a qualified veterinary surgeon and will produce a receipted account within six months in respect of the operation.

5 The keeper will maintain at his own expense an annual vaccination programme as advised by a veterinary surgeon.

6 The keeper hereby irrevocably authorises a representative of the Shelter at any time to enter any enclosure or building where the horse is kept for the purpose of inspecting the horse or its surroundings, or for the purpose of repossessing the horse in accordance with Clause 11 of these conditions.

7 The keeper will notify the Shelter of any change of address where the animal is being kept.

8 The keeper will at his own expense purchase any necessary licence or permit for the horse.

9 Whilst every endeavour is made that the horse is healthy when leaving the Shelter (unless otherwise stated) no guarantee can be given that the horse will not manifest or develop sickness or diseases thereafter, and the Shelter accepts no liability for any diseases or defect in health or temperament whatsoever that the horse may later be found to suffer. The Shelter should be notified.

10 The keeper shall not part with possession of the horse without the prior written permission of the Shelter.

11 Should the keeper fail to comply in any way with the terms of this agreement or if for any reason whatever an official of the Shelter considers it to be in the interest of the horse to do so, the Shelter may forthwith and without notice recover possession of the horse in which event the above-named keeper's rights will cease.

Horse sales

There are always plenty of horses on offer at a horse sale, and they are widely advertised, ranging from the famous bloodstock sales at Newmarket and High Performance sales at Stoneleigh, to more local and regular sales such as those at Leicester and Cambridge. Wherever you live, you should be able to find at least one sale within easy travelling distance.

Advantages of buying from a horse sale

● There will be a large selection of animals to view in one place.

● You will pay the actual market price on the day.

● There will be conditions of sale to safeguard both the purchaser and vendor.

● A veterinary panel may be in attendance to check the horse if required.

● If the horse is found not to conform to its warranty, it can be returned within a certain time.

Disadvantages of buying from a horse sale

● Depending on the sale, you may see horses and ponies being bought up for the meat market.

● You need to be unsympathetic to all the horses that are not going to be suitable for you.

● It will be very easy to bid for a horse because you feel sorry for it.

● Sometimes you may get run up on a horse and end up paying more than the animal is worth to secure it.

● Catalogue claims by the vendors may not be quite accurate.

Sales know-how

● If you do go to a sale with the intention of buying a horse, make sure you take someone with you who is familiar with auction procedure.

● Study the conditions of sale carefully, as they are fully and comprehensively printed out.

● Keep your hands firmly in your pocket unless you mean to bid.

● Avoid the auctioneer's eye unless you mean to bid.

● Do not get caught napping if you want to buy.

● Some lots may be missing or sold very quickly, so get in place early.

● Secure a place under the auctioneer's nose so that he does not miss you.

● Give your name clearly and loudly.

● If you are not known to the auctioneer, do not forget to make prior arrangements for payment.

A gift horse

A real gift horse can be a lovely surprise or a total disaster, depending on the reasons for the gift.

Advantages of a gift horse

● No financial outlay.

● Often an unexpected joy.

● May be the horse you have always dreamed of.

Disadvantages of a gift horse

● It may be a gift only because there is something wrong with it.

● It may not be offered with the best of motives.

● The owner may just be looking to get rid of the horse without having the guts to put it down themselves, and hope someone else will do the dirty work for them.

● There may be imminent heavy vets bills.

● It may be dangerous and unridable.

As you can see, the success of a gift horse depends on the motives of the donor. A well-intentioned present would be wonderful, any other motives calamitous.

Chance encounters

Some chance encounters have been known to have the happiest of conclusions, while others may be just a waste of time. As you drive round the area, keep an eye open when passing horses to see if there is one you really like the look of.

If you do locate such an animal, it should not be too difficult to place it under surveillance to see if it is being used or not, or to locate the owner to find if the animal could in fact be for sale.

Many owners, even if they had no intention of selling the horse, would be flattered to think that someone liked it enough to try to buy it. However, do make sure that you do not keep lurking in the background and give the impression that you are a scout for a horse thief.

Show encounters

Show encounters can be far better engineered than chance encounters, and there will be a great many horses on view, even if they are not ostensibly for sale.

If you are looking for a showjumper, go to a jumping show. If you want a show horse, have a look round the show rings. Eventers will be seen in action at events, gymkhana ponies at gymkhanas. If you want a horse to take to shows, then these are very good places to find the horse that want doing its job, without enduring a lot of old sales talk first.

If you see a horse that takes your fancy, approach the rider to find out if it is available. You are strongly advised to pick your moment wisely, as the most even-tempered people can be irritable and not want to be bothered when they are trying to concentrate.

Most secretary's offices at venues where shows are regularly held will have an ad board on which people can advertise horses for sale, and the secretary will often also be able to help by giving you names or phone numbers where you could contact riders later.

If you are a good rider, you may wish to look for a horse that is not going well, with the intention of improving it and bringing out its full potential. You could catch the owner in a mood to get rid of it and the price may be a little lower than on a good day. However, do not be too clever and underestimate the jockey on top. It is entirely possible that you may be able to do no better, so be extremely honest with yourself about your capabilities.

If you are not a particularly experienced rider, you should be looking for a horse that is doing its job kindly in a quiet workmanlike manner. It should be presenting its jockey with *no* resistance in any shape or form.

A horse that has a main ambition to return to the lorry park is certainly not the right one to choose to buy, even for a more experienced rider, as one method of napping will soon lead to other types of try-on. Far simpler to avoid this sort of argument unless you are a very strong jockey and want to buy the horse dirt cheap.

At one recent BSJA show, a rider was helped by her mother on the ground with a hunting whip which was waved at the animal every time it came round the end of the practice ring which was closest to the horse boxes. When the horse actually went into the ring to jump, mother stood threateningly at the entrance. The horse jumped a clear round, but should never be thought suitable to be bought by a novice family.

Whatever type of horse you want to buy, you should be able to see it in action somewhere - check out the horsy press for details of shows to be held in the near future. Riding Club and Pony Club shows are often good places to see a wide variety of types of classes, and also therefore types of horses.

Have a clear idea of what you are looking for so you do not get lured to another ringside to change all your expectations and plans on impulse.

Shows provide a wonderful opportunity to view the horses when they are out at work, rather than at home, and you will have a much clearer picture of their behaviour. Most vendors should be honest enough not to misrepresent their horse's ability, but at home this can often be disguised, and it is up to you to decipher how much of the glowing description is accurate and unbiased.

At a show you will be able to decide for yourself with the evidence of the horse's behaviour and ability before your very eyes.

However, even at shows, owners can still take a very biased attitude to their horse's prowess, and seem oblivious to how everyone else views it. It is a total waste of time for a rider to describe her horse as a potential winner if the whole showground has seen it stop three times at the first fence; but if you had not been there yourself, you might have believed a hard-luck story to explain why it had not won first prize for showjumping.

The judges didn't really prefer a finer type in the hunter ring. He was rather handicapped because he refused to leave the corner by the collecting ring, and reared up every time the steward tried to lead it away. Another missed rosette! Still, it was certainly worth going to watch and disprove another myth.

Traffic problems could have explained why the horse was too late to enter the Riding Horse class. What a good job you were there to help load it up to go home again - it only took three hours for the 'perfect in every way' horse to get back in the trailer. Such a pity it broke the ramp spring in the process!

And did you see that horse in the collecting ring with a green ribbon in its tail to show that it was a baby and not to be crowded? From the mayhem it caused, surely the red one warning of a kicker would have been more appropriate.

If you are looking for a working hunter horse, go to a show and watch the horses in action. Perhaps the one that catches your eye is for sale.

If you want to showjump seriously, your horse will have to jump water. Even if he sails over the second time of asking, you will still have collected 3 faults. Is this something you feel you can overcome? Might it always come between you and a clear round? Do you want to go to a show hoping that the water jump will be omitted?

Are you prepared to overlook the fact that the horse may be a reluctant loader?

There are endless examples of owners being caught out in their exaggerated claims, or in the sins of omission. They won't mention the eliminations, the dressage scores in the 90s, the 'cricket scores' for showjumping, the napping in the show ring and the refusal to pass umbrellas when out hacking.

While this is not quite dishonest, it is getting pretty close. If you have any suspicions at all that they may be evasive about telling the whole truth, do not proceed with the deal until you have checked the animal out.

Similarly, examine your own credentials. Are you sure you have given the owner an accurate impression about your own capabilities? Do not try to con the owner into thinking you are better (or worse!) than you are. Be frank about the kind of home your new horse will have, and offer to let your premises or livery yard be inspected. If the owner thinks the horse is not going to be suitable for you, let them

have the opportunity to say so, and do not brush their opinions to one side. This is why so many horses change hands very quickly.

Right for the job
An enthusiastic but fairly incompetent rider contacted a dealer to find a horse with which to go hunting. He wanted a nice sharp 17-hands thoroughbred horse capable of winning in the show ring, perfect in traffic, to go first or last in the field, and to be up with the master at the end of the day.

He had enough funds to afford this type of animal, and the dealer had just the horse in the yard, so an appointment was made.

In the meantime, the dealer had a phone call from a friend asking if the gentleman had been in touch. He was extremely amused to find out which horse had been ear-

Above right This horse may be described as a good cross-country performer, but you would not be able to do this at a show!

Right Okay for the pairs class, though!

162

This rider is enjoying her horse's high spirits, but perhaps it will be too lively for you. Don't overestimate your skills!

marked to be shown off, and suggested a drastic review.

Although the gentleman could well afford a nice horse, he certainly was not able to ride one of such calibre. This supposed hard-hunting, all-day enthusiast was well known for attending the meet, jogging along behind, and being a marvellous organiser and fund-raiser for the Hunt Supporters Club. He was always ready to go home after two hours, and had never been out all day. The social aspects of the Hunt appealed to him, and he was very good at them, but not the riding.

His present horse was a barrel-like cob with impeccable manners who was getting a little elderly for the job. The cob was also rather plain, if not downright ugly, in the head and the gentleman obviously felt the time had arrived to cut more of a dash.

The dealer was very relieved to hear all this before the gentleman arrived, as the horse he had planned to show needed a good rider. Fortunately he also had to hand a lovely little cob mare, clean legs and a very pretty head. She was also most affectionate and willing, and totally 'bombproof'. When the gentleman arrived, the dealer was relieved to see he was a little short in the leg, just the correct size for the little mare. No mention was made of showy thoroughbreds as the mare was led out of her stable. If the gentleman was disappointed to see her it did not show. He *was completely taken by her pretty face and generous, kind eye. He watched her being ridden and saw her pop a few cross-country fences, and obviously could not wait to get on board himself.*

The dealer thought the gentleman's wife looked distinctly relieved to see such a nice little horse presented to her husband, so she must have been aware of his somewhat limited ability in the saddle. The mare did all that the gentleman asked of her and was bought on the spot.

Several years on he is still enchanted with her, and she has a lovely home where she is certainly not overworked.

There are two lessons to be learned. First, do not ask for more than you are capable of managing, in case it is found for you. Second, do not blame the dealer if you cannot cope with the horse you have asked for.

This latter circumstance is one of the reasons why dealers sometimes get a poor reputation. The buyer overestimates his ability, cannot cope with what he has bought, and has to return it. He then blames the dealer for selling him a wrong 'un. Talk straight to the dealer and he will generally be straight with you. After all, it is his reputation that suffers when people find out where an unsuitable horse has come from.

One last warning before the next step to horse ownership! Beware the horse that is impeccably behaved but in poor condition. Reasons like 'He's just come off the boat' or 'He's been rescued from a bad home' to explain the lack of flesh may well be true. It may also be true that when the horse recovers condition, it turns into a demon, and needs to be kept poor to be manageable.

5
BUYING PROCEDURES

OKAY, the horse is found. Now let's take a look at what happens next.

Price

First sort out the price! If that being asked is more than you can afford, ask the owners if they will be prepared to talk, that is negotiate or haggle. If they are definitely not open to offers, the sensible course is to proceed no further. If you really like the horse but cannot afford it, it will colour your view of other horses to be viewed in the near future, so leave well alone.

However, it will still be worth leaving your phone number in case they are unable to sell it for the price required, and are more prepared to listen, but do not set too much store on it. It is only very occasionally that a real live bargain is found, as we saw in an earlier chapter, and you have to be in exactly the right place at the right time to take advantage of such an opportunity. You must also have a strong nerve!

Search for another horse that is definitely in your price range, not forgetting, of course, that most vendors ask more for the horse than they are prepared to accept. You will therefore have to indulge in a little horse-trading yourself, but as long as the starting price is close to your top limit, you will stand a chance of securing the goods.

Avoid disclosing your top limit to the vendor if the price of the horse has yet to be mentioned. For certain, the price then asked will be pitched just a little higher to give you scope to bargain it down again. You will never find a horse below your top limit once you have admitted what that limit is. If you are a naturally straightforward person, it will be difficult to assume this devious sort of attitude, but it can certainly save you money in the event of a sale being agreed.

What sort of money? This will be the first thing a dealer will want to know when he is contacted about buying a horse. Try to wriggle out of admitting a firm limit, saying that you will be prepared to pay around such-and-such for the right horse - always pitch it on the lower side to give you more scope. If the dealer laughs and puts the phone down, you know you have pitched a bit too low for the sort of horse you have asked for.

You may have to phone back with a higher range if everyone you contact hangs up on you, but if you cannot afford the sort of prices the vendors are expecting actually to get, both dealers or private individuals, then set your sights a little lower. It is no good paying more than you can afford for a horse because you will not be able to look after it properly. You can fool and bluff a lot of people in the horse world, but not your bank manager, and eventually not your family either.

Never forget, anyway, that you cannot buy success, so if you are ambitious, look for the less experienced animal that will take more time to come right. Spend time on it instead of more money for a more advanced horse.

When you have found a suitable-sounding horse in your price range, what next?

Viewing

The next stage is to arrange a viewing. Try not to leave it too long before you go to examine the horse

Above right When viewing your prospective purchase, check for any obvious blemishes. If you find something that you do not like, it could save you the cost of the vetting.

Right Your vet is not going to like an obviously enlarged hock like this.

Far right Even if you know nothing about horse's teeth, you can tell by the length of those shown here that they obviously do not belong to a youngster.

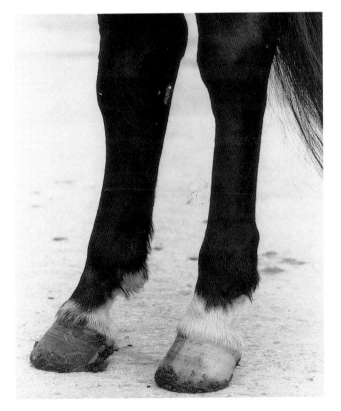

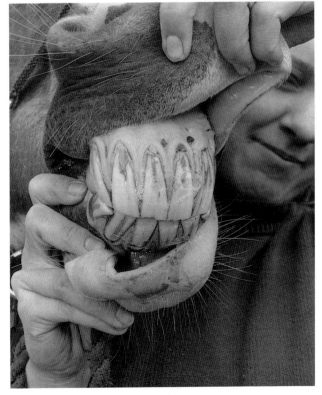

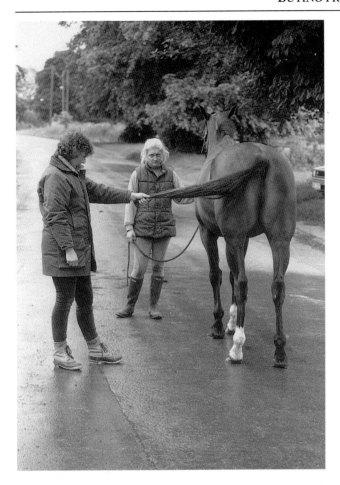

Are the hind legs a good matching pair?

This sand crack has obviously had some attention from the farrier, but the crack still extends up into the coronary band. It is likely to remain, so could it be a reason for rejecting the horse?

at its stables - you would be absolutely amazed at the things that can go wrong between you fixing a viewing and actually turning up to do so.

As mentioned earlier, turn up early on the appointed day. This does not have to mean that you are trying to catch them out - you can put it down to keenness, but if they are not being quite straight with you it is well to be aware of this before dealing commences.

First check the horse over carefully to make sure it fits the description of the one you have turned up to see. One vendor was away at a show when some purchasers turned up to see a horse.

The groom showed them the wrong horse, unfortunately a more valuable animal, and there was a lot of bad feeling as both sides felt they were in the right. The purchasers wanted the better horse at the lower horse's price, despite the mistake being explained. The owner did not mind selling the better horse, but naturally wanted more money for it than the price

Left Ask to see the horse led up on a hard surface. Is he willing to trot freely?

originally quoted for the lesser animal. No deal done! Before you get enthusiastic about trying the horse, look it over in the stable to make sure that there are no obvious blemishes that will cause your vet to spin the animal straight away. This could save you a full vetting fee.

Next ask to see the animal led up in hand on a hard surface. If you do not know why this should be procedure, make sure you are accompanied by a friend or adviser who does know what to be looking out for. Your vet will not like

- Too close an action in front or behind

- Stiffness on first coming out of the stable or field

- Pigeon toes

- Unequal or asymmetrical feet

- Sand cracks or other blemishes to the horn which may not be so apparent in the field or stable,

You might wish to see the horse loose-schooled over a fence. This one has a very cheeky attitude - he looks as if he wants to do it! He has lots of spring. . .tucks his hind feet up nicely. . .lands well out from the fence and really means to clear it. But will he jump as well with someone on top? Nice to watch, but not the truest of tests.

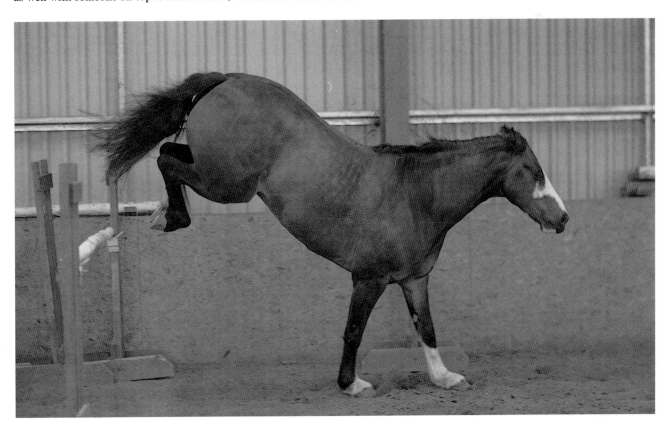

Opposite Do not be too inflexible and insist on buying a snaffle-mouthed horse. As long as the horse behaves as nicely as this and is quite comfortable in his mouth, give him a chance to please you.

Above Many cobs are ridden in a pelham as they may be too strong for an average rider to control with a snaffle.

particularly rings round the foot which would indicate a history and tendency to laminitis

• Actual lameness. Do not be fobbed off by the story of the horse needing the blacksmith. This could be true, but decent shoeing might not alleviate the problem. Offer to return when the blacksmith has just been.

Do not be afraid at this stage to say what you think. If there is a blemish or anything else like dishing or brushing that you will find hard to live with, be honest about it. Do not go through the motions of trying the horse under saddle if you now have no intention of buying it - it just is not fair to horse or owner.

If all is still okay, before the horse is tacked up you might wish to see it loose-schooled over a fence. While this gives an indication of the horse's attitude to jumping, it does not follow that the horse will jump as well when impeded by a jockey. Nice to watch, but not the truest of tests.

If you now want to see the horse ridden, ask to see it tacked up. A horse described as 'snaffle-mouthed' should now be kitted out in a snaffle. If the owner produces a pelham or other type of bit suggestive of the horse being strong, be wary. It is just possible that the owner might consider you too weedy for his horse and wants to ensure your safety. But if the owner thinks it is *you* who needs the pelham, perhaps *you* will always need to ride the horse in such a bit, even if the horse really was snaffle-mouthed with a better rider. Weigh it up!

An element of caution should never be absent when buying a horse. Disappointing and repetitive though it sounds, buying the wrong horse is a far more traumatic experience than buying the wrong car or motorbike. By the time you have discovered that the horse is not quite right for the job, you will probably have grown fond of it and parting will be doubly difficult.

173

Above left Insist on seeing the horse ridden before you get on it - don't get on it first. Apart from the safety factor, you should want to see what it looks like under saddle, and how strongly it needs to be ridden.

Left Is the trot active and level?

Above Is there any reluctance to accelerate?

Right When galloping, is there any abnormal breathing sound? Does the horse show any tendency to hot up?

Returning to the viewing procedure, insist on seeing the horse ridden before you get on it unless you know the horse and owner very well. Accidents can happen and it should be to the vendor's benefit to show how well the horse is capable of going before the prospective purchaser gets on board. This is a sensible procedure to follow to ensure that the horse is given a fair chance to perform to the best of its ability.

Without hurrying, ask to see the horse walked, trotted, cantered and galloped, paying special attention to its willingness to be obedient and cooperative both when going forward and slowing down. Listen out at this stage to the horse's breathing in case the animal sounds distressed - the vet will certainly take note of any excessive noise the horse makes.

If the horse shows any sign of napping, bucking, rearing or general bad behaviour, decide to what degree this is acceptable. Unless you are a better rider than the owner, the horse will be unlikely to improve under you.

If all is well and you are buying the horse to go jumping, ask to see the animal perform. Do not ask too much in size to start with, rather study the animal's technique over the pole. Does it get excited and become strong, or is it reluctant to go forwards? If it has been advertised as an exceptional jumper

easily clearing 5 feet, now is the time for the owner to put his money where his mouth is and demonstrate this wonderful creature's true capabilities.

If the claims about its ability have been exaggerated, do not let it put you off if you do not need your horse to be quite so high-powered. Just make sure its limitations are reflected when the time comes to finalise the price.

If you have reached the stage where everything so far is okay, get on the horse yourself. Give the horse plenty of time to adjust to someone fresh and move off quietly, sorting out the reins and stirrups before you go.

Only when you are completely comfortable should you ask the horse to start to perform. It is advisable to carry out the same sequence of exercise you have just watched so you can mentally compare things with you riding, and your friend and adviser can do the same from the sidelines.

If you feel at home on the horse after working at all paces, and it has done nothing to make you feel wary, then you are ready to try it out for the specific job or jobs you have in mind. If you want to jump, jump it. If dressage is your particular interest, begin to work it collectedly. If you mean to event, check both, and try to find out the horse's attitude to cross country-fences. If you want to ride on the road, ask

Above left Ears pricked and hind feet well tucked up indicate that this horse knows and enjoys his job.

Above This horse is obviously concerned about the change of rider.

Right Five minutes later, both horse and rider have started to relax.

the owner to ride it up the road first so you can see for yourself how it behaves with traffic.

There may be no adequate facilities with which to try the horse at the owner's establishment, so if you really like the horse, ask if you can try it out somewhere else. Many riding establishments hire out their facilities as a training ground, so locate the nearest suitable place and book. Assure the owner that you will be responsible for the expenses incurred in such an outing, both in hiring fees and the transport. If the owner is reluctant to let the horse be tried elsewhere, it is possible that he is afraid it will go badly, so adjust your attitude accordingly.

If you want to do hunter trials, you really do need to see for yourself that the horse will go through water and over ditches, always the big stoppers. You also need to be assured that the horse will settle and concentrate in an unfamiliar place. Even if the horse is destined only for light hacking, it is still sensible to reassure yourself that it will go willingly where it is pointed, not try to nap home, back to the lorry or to other horses.

So, the horse of your dreams has been found! You are 101 per cent certain that it is the one for you, so what next? Try to avoid giving a direct commitment immediately. It will be far better for you to discuss the horse privately at home and ring back later with your decision and your offer. Breathing space in horse deals must not be underestimated, and might prevent you making a silly offer that you will later regret.

You will have to reach agreement on a price. Do not be pushed into making a hasty offer by the vendor's seeming reluctance to deal, and mentions of other interested parties. You will know how much you can afford, and also how much the horse is worth to you personally. Don't forget, if you *really* want the horse and have to pay a bit more than you would *prefer*, do not lose it over a few pounds. You will spend far more than that in travel and time looking for something else suitable.

If you cannot *afford* to pay more, then be resigned to not buying it and look for something cheaper. If you are so far adrift on price that a bit of give and take will not meet in the middle, you might have been wiser to have stayed away in the first place.

As has already been pointed out several times, real bargains are rare, although not unheard of, so it is worth trying your luck with a low offer and seeing what sort of response is forthcoming. If the owners are desperate to sell, it could pay off, but do not bank on it.

If the price is agreed, then comes the really tricky bit.

Vetting

You have already seen that it could be difficult to sort out which vet to use, but eventually you will find one acceptable to all parties.

If you are worried about the outcome, you will be better off not to attend the examination. You will know soon enough if you are paying up or still on the lookout. If you do wish to attend, vets go through a fairly standard procedure recommended by the Royal College of Veterinary Surgeons and the British Veterinary Association.

In the stable, the vet will check eyes, heart, breathing, and legs and feet for anything obviously wrong. The horse will then be run up in hand, and if all is still well, ridden or worked strenuously. Any signs of lameness or faulty action will be noted, and heart and breathing will again be checked. The horse will then be rested before the final trot up.

If the vet is suspicious of anything sinister, he may ask to X-ray the horse, and it will be up to you how

Above left If you are buying the horse to jump, then jump it. But do not forget that when you ask the horse to react to you, he will be unfamiliar with your signals. Give him enough time to settle to do his job.

This page Horse and rider are soon coming to terms with each other.

far the examination should go. You are strongly advised to have a blood test done in case the horse is on painkillers to mask any infirmity. You will receive a certificate from the vet stating what he has found, and his opinion as to the suitability of the horse for its intended use.

The vet is not going to say 'Pass' or 'Fail'. You must tell him what particular work you are buying the horse for, and he will be able to tell you his opinion as to its suitability healthwise. On the standard examination form, there is a section to be filled in stating the vet's opinion. He will be able to say he has found no defects likely to affect the horse's job, or that there are defects as noted but that they will be unlikely to cause problems for a particular job. Conversely, he will also be able to say that he feels the animal will be unsuitable for what you want it to do.

If, in the course of the vetting, some blemish or defect is discovered, do not be shy about asking for a price reduction. You might need that reduction to pay for the vet to put the defect right. If you want the vet's opinion on how much the horse is costing, ask him if he thinks it is worth it. He is certainly in the business to have a good idea of the sort of prices horses are fetching. If you do not want him to know the price, you are not obliged to tell him. Don't forget -

that should already have been settled between you and the vendor.

If the vet considers the horse to be okay, you are home and dry, with only the paperwork to sort out. Get the vaccination certificates, passport and any registration papers in your possession and then part with the money. If you do it the other way round, you might find that any papers are a long time coming. If the horse is going to be insured, do it before you hand the money over. A million and one things could go wrong between buying it and fetching it home, so it is essential to be covered.

Even if the horse is considered to be unsuitable, you could of course still buy it against the vet's advice, but you would be most unwise. Spare a thought for the owner in this eventuality, as he is now left with a horse that is not going to be quite so easy to pass on. Some owners take this failure quite lightly, and you might wonder if they suspected something amiss all the time. Others go berserk, taking the vet's opinion as a personal slur, and are very unpleasant and rude. Take it with a pinch of salt. Remember, it is a situation you can walk away from with only disappointment and the cost of the vetting to bear - it is the owner will now be stuck with a horse known to have been spun in that particular vet or owner's area.

6
A HORSE OF YOUR OWN

THE BIG day has arrived, the horse has passed the veterinary examination with flying colours, and there is now nothing to prevent you entering a new phase of your life as a *horse owner*.

What do you do next?

The first thing is to make arrangements to pay. Also, if you are going to insure the horse, do so at once while the animal is not quite yours. You should certainly insure the horse before it leaves its original home, just in case accidents occur when loading or travelling.

Either collect the horse yourself, or preferably have it delivered in its usual lorry or trailer. It will be far less traumatic for the animal to be established in its new home if it has not been fretting all the way because the transport is different.

When the horse arrives, be very careful that it does not get off to a bad start. Have a nice feed waiting for it. Put it into its new stable, or paddock if it is on its own, and leave it in peace to get its bearings and settle down. If it is going to have to share a field with other horses, make sure that all the others are out of the field to start with so it can explore its new boundaries without being harassed.

When the horse has familiarised itself with the field, try to present its companions in a sensible manner. Introduce it first to the least aggressive horse in the field and put them in together. Pray that they will not fight! If it can pal up with one of the horses before meeting the whole group it stands a better chance of keeping out of trouble.

If you can put it in an adjacent field for a few days so that it can socialise safely, so much the better, but of course, this may not be possible - it will depend on the circumstances of your livery. Removal of the hind shoes is a sensible move, but unless the other horses belong to you, not practical. Other owners are unlikely to co-operate to such an extent. At some stage you are going to have to take the chance and let your horse loose in its new home and establish its own pecking order.

If things are intolerable in a shared paddock, and your horse is getting beaten up, or beating up the others, ask the owner of the establishment if you can fence off part of the field at your own expense. If this is not acceptable, you will have to consider moving elsewhere or keeping the horse in a stable most of the time. This could work if you were able to manage to turn your horse out earlier or later than the others to avoid a clash.

Of course, you may be lucky and find that the horses all get along well together, and there are some simple rules to stick to if they are going to stay compatible:

- Never give your horse titbits if the other horses can see. Jealousy and greed *must* be avoided.

- Never try to feed your horse in the same field as the others. It will lead to fighting, and you may get damaged if you try to stand guard.

- Always try to feed your horse at the same time as its neighbours. If you are all arriving at different times, try to establish some sort of rota so that all the horses are fed at the same time.

- Do not try to groom when the other horses are being fed, even if yours has already eaten. Wait until the yard has settled down.

- If the horses are all tearing around and being silly, do not persist in trying to catch yours until they have settled down. It will be a waste of time and you might be injured.

- Be extra careful taking your horse in and out of the field to avoid a melee at the gate.

An 'only' horse will not be damaged by other horses asserting their authority, but you may have the problem of the horse being lonely, particularly if it has been used to company. It will be quite distressing to hear it calling for its friends, but unfortunately it will just have to get used to its new situation. You will be able to help it settle quite quickly with a bit of common-sense:

- Try to quarter it where it will be able to see plenty of activity, and pop in and out to reassure it.

- Resist the temptation to borrow a pony for a few days as a companion. Things will be just as bad when the pony has to go back.

- Do not be *at* the horse all the time to try to compensate for its loss. You won't be able to keep it up.

- Try to establish a routine as quickly as possible and stick to it. Your new horse will find it reassuring if he receives his meals on time.

- Mucking out, grooming and exercising should also follow a routine which you will be able to maintain consistently.

- Try to avoid the horse becoming bored, and include lots of changes of scenery when you ride out.

- Check your fencing - you cannot be sure that the horse will not try to jump out if it hears another horse go by.

- Make sure the horse has enough exercise and resist the urge to overfeed it as a 'comfort'. You will soon make it snappy if it has too many tit-bits.

The horse will soon settle down, particularly if his circumstances may have changed for the better. Just keep a sympathetic eye on him to make sure he does not pine too badly, and wait for him to cheer up. A well-kept horse has no cause for complaint, and you should soon recognise the character you found attractive enough to buy.

Your horse's diet

It is a sensible idea to find out from the previous owner what your new horse has been used to eating. You need to know:

- what make of food, eg Spillers, Baileys, Dodson & Horrell, etc

- what type of food, eg coarse mix (whether it is non-heating pasture mix, a performance mix or a general horse and pony mix) or cubes or whether

he has been fed on straights (ie, oats, barley, etc)

- how much (in pounds or kgs not in handfuls or scoops)

Try to keep your horse on his usual diet during the transition from one home to another and for a short while afterwards. This will avoid stressing him unduly and give you the chance to review whether or not there is any need to change the horse's diet.

The amount and type of food your horse receives will be dependent upon many factors:

Current bodyweight and condition

As a general rule horses and ponies are fed around 2.5% of their bodyweight as their total daily ration; for example, if a horse weighs 500 kg he will receive 12.5 kg per day. The secret with feeding is to treat each horse as an individual.

You can find out your horse's bodyweight by

- using the table below, which is very much a general guide only

- by taking a couple of measurements and using the formula detailed below

- by using one of the equi-measuring tapes which enable you to read off the horse's bodyweight and expected daily intake

- or by taking the horse to a public weighbridge (if there is one handy to your stables).

Approximate bodyweights

Height	Type	Weight (lbs/kg)
14.2	pony	990/450
14.2	cob	1100/500
15	hack	990/450
16	Thoroughbred	1210/550
16	hunter	1320/600
16.2	hunter	1430/650

Bodyweight (lbs) = $\dfrac{\text{heart girth (in) squared x length}}{241}$

or

Bodyweight (kg) = $\dfrac{\text{heart girth (cm) squared x length}}{8717}$

The other factor you need to consider is the horse's condition. Is he too fat? Too thin? Or just about right? Your objectives for the horse, in terms of weight gain, loss or maintenance, will have a bearing on the type of feedstuffs you use.

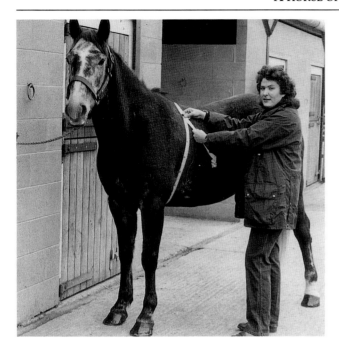

Using a special tape to determine a horse's bodyweight and daily food requirement.

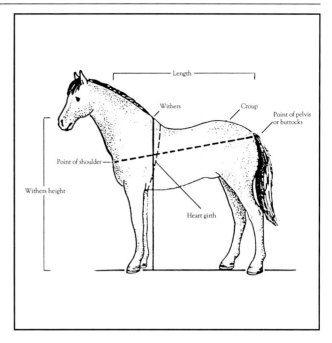

Diagram showing where to measure a horse's heart girth, withers height, and length.

Age, temperament and breeding

Horses' nutritional needs vary according to their age and stage of growth. For instance, foals need more and better quality protein because of the rate of their bone and muscle growth; old horses need food that can be easily chewed; while in the last three months of pregnancy mares have increased protein needs.

Some horses become a little too lively if fed foods such as oats, other animals become fat very easily and need their food intake carefully managed, whilst yet others appear to eat great amounts yet still manage to look lean. Your horse's type and breeding plays a part here - cobs, for instance, generally do well on comparatively little, whereas a highly strung Thoroughbred type may need much more just to keep its weight stable.

If the horse is a 'worrier' then weight may easily be lost - or perhaps you own a fussy feeder who picks away showing little interest in what is in the feed bucket. Such problems cannot be ignored - you need to tailor the diet to suit each horse's individual needs and 'quirks'.

Workload

In order simply to stay alive and maintain his bodyweight the horse needs a certain amount of food, which is known as his maintenance diet. However, if we want the horse to work, he will need extra food, but exactly how much depends on the type of work; for example, light hacking is nowhere near as strenu-

ous as showjumping, which in turn is not as demanding as hunting all day.

The total amount of food a horse is given each day will also be split into hay and concentrates, with the proportion of concentrates increasing as the workload increases. A horse that is resting or just on walking exercise could get all he needed from hay alone. If, however, the horse was being schooled and jumped regularly, his work would generally be regarded as being of medium severity and the split would be 60 per cent of the daily ration coming from hay and 40 per cent coming from concentrate feeds.

The maxim is always to feed according to the amount of work done - there is no point in having a horse stuffed full of high-energy foods if he is not going to be worked properly. Over-feeding can lead to all kinds of problems with both thehealth and behaviour of the horse.

The quality of the feed also comes into play - poor hay will have a minimal feed value, and apart from that should be avoided as it is likely to be dusty, which will give your horse other problems. Feed only good-quality foodstuffs and keep them in vermin-proof containers. You can see from the feed bags when the sell-by date is, so check that you are not buying old stock and that you will be able to use the contents before the date stipulated.

Past history

If the horse has a history of problems such as laminitis or azoturia you would be well advised to consult

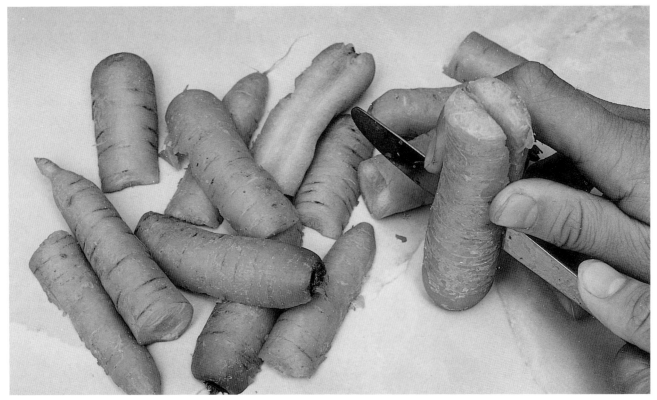

Far left Dengie products have been used with success for animals with laminitis. They are also used for ordinary horses and ponies.

Left 'Horsehage' is one of the product names for dust-free hay. Other makes are available.

Below left The correct way to slice carrots in order to feed them safely to horses.

Right Feed companies make a variety of ready-prepared foods and often provide free nutritional advice to horse owners as well.

an equine nutritionist and gain their advice on products to use. The feed companies also usually have their own experts who can recommend diets or advice can also be sought via such as the Horse Answers section and panel of experts in *Your Horse* magazine.

If you buy a horse with respiratory problems, you can expect your feed and bedding bills to be higher: at the least your horse will need soaked hay, at worst he may need one of the specially prepared 'haylages', which are obviously more expensive than hay. They do, however, have the advantage that as they have high nutritional values, often your concentrate feed can be reduced.

Straw beds are out for respiratory cases: instead, more expensive paper, shavings or Aubiose beds will be required. Rubber matting is also a possibility - the initial investment will be outweighed by the long life of good rubber stable flooring.

Water

This is a vital requirement for life - horses can survive for longer without food than they can without water. It is essential that your horse has clean, fresh water available at all times. They generally drink around 10 gallons a day - if their drinking or eating pattern changes in any way, you should check for other signs of something being wrong (see the Signs of Health and Disease section on page 14).

Other points to remember

- Keep a record of your horse's weight - use the same method to check the bodyweight each

time and record it on a fortnightly basis so you know exactly what is happening.

- Use succulents such as apples and carrots to add interest to the horse's food and to tempt fussy eaters.

- Horses are designed to be grazing for 12-16 hours every day - if we alter their lifestyle to suit ours, by keeping them confined in stables and limiting their grazing time, we have to ensure they do not suffer and become bored. Hay needs to be provided at regular intervals.

- The horse's stomach is intended to always be half-full, so we must arrange their lifestyle and feeds to follow nature as closely as possible. Keeping a horse stabled and providing hay only in the morning and last thing at night is not good enough. Horses turned out to graze are happier, but you have to remember that there is very little goodness in the grass from October through the winter until the spring months. Grazing therefore needs to be supplemented by hay throughout this time.

The healthy horse

In order to keep your horse happy and healthy you need to reproduce his natural lifestyle as much as possible. Horses were designed to roam free, grazing for 12-16 hours a day and keeping company with their own kind. Yet we impose confinement upon them, ensuring they spend hours in their stables, on their own, feeding them at times we find convenient.

While you obviously need to accommodate your personal circumstances, do try and give your horse the best possible lifestyle.

Suggested daily routines.

● Organise a routine, as horses like this - it represents security to them to know when they are going out in the field, when they are to be fed, etc. They have an in-built clock and your horse will soon let you know if you are late giving him breakfast!

● Turn them out with other equine company for as much of the day as possible. In winter you need to ensure he is warm and protected from the elements (through the provision of rugs, field shelters, adequate natural hedging to give shelter) and that he has hay and water. In summer he will need protection from the sun (shelters/hedges) and flies (there are many fly-repellents on the market) and plenty of water.

● Follow the golden rules of feeding: feed your horse little and often (which imitates nature); give plenty of bulk (again following nature's requirement); and provide succulents.

● Ensure that your horse's stable is large enough for him, high enough so that he does not injure his head if he jerks back, and is well ventilated.

● Handle your horse with quiet confidence and smooth movements. You will make him jumpy if you are rushing in and out, swinging buckets around, etc.

● Respect the fact that many animals like to be left in peace to eat their feed. You cannot really blame him if he gets tetchy because you insist on grooming his tickly bits while he's having tea.

● Read as much as you can about equine behaviour; it is only by knowing your own horse and understanding the language by which he communicates that you can recognise when things are starting to go wrong. For instance, a change in behaviour can be brought about by the horse being in pain. Obvious changes are easy to recognise - it is the subtle changes that you need to be aware of and need to act upon.

● Give your horse adequate work. Most of them do not enjoy being stuck in the same field for month after month doing absolutely nothing.

● If you discover you have made a mistake and cannot cope with a horse, then do the right thing by the animal and find him the best possible home.

Calling the vet

If things are clearly not right, or if you are in any doubt, it is always best to call out the vet. Certainly call him:

● If the horse is in obvious pain or distress.

● If the horse collapses.

● If a wound is bleeding badly and the flow of blood cannot be controlled by pressure. Should the blood be bright red it means that the horse is bleeding from an artery - it will spurt from the wound in time with the heart beat. Emergency veterinary attention should be sought immediately.

● If you think that a bone has been broken or a tendon or ligament strained.

● When a wound is so deep that it has penetrated through the layers of skin and will require stitching.

● If a horse's normal rates - pulse, temperature and respiration - have altered for no apparent reason.

● When a contagious disease is suspected.

● If colic or laminitis is suspected.

● If a wound is deep and the horse has not recently had a tetanus jab.

● If a horse is off food for more than 24 hours.

● If the animal coughs repeatedly.

● If the horse is suddenly lame for no apparent reason.

Some conditions worsen considerably with time; for example, within an hour of the first signs of laminitis some serious anatomical changes are taking place within the horse's foot, so the earlier the treatment, the better.

Worming

Parasites are the enemies of all horses - and as a caring owner it is vital you operate a regular worming programme. If you do not take simple measures, you put your horse in danger; at the least a horse suffering from a parasite burden will not thrive, while at worst parasites can cause death.

Horses need to be wormed right from being six-week-

Equine first aid kit

What it should contain and why

Veterinary thermometer (available from saddlers).

Vaseline - for greasing the thermometer.

Several different sizes of bowls - used for preparing poultices, for holding saline solution.

Dinsfectant - for sterlising bowls.

Bandages - crepe, elasticated, stable. A selection will be needed, and you may need to use several at the same time. There are also ready-made bandages designed to keep dressings secure in awkward places.

A selection of dressings - eg, gamgee, gauze, non-stick.

Poultices - ready-made ones can be bought, eg Animalintex, and there are also herbal ones available now. Used to draw out infection.

Wound powder - antiseptic powder in 'puffer' containers or spray-on containers. There are also oils, eg green oils, which are ideal for horses that need protection but which live out so ordinary wound powders would soon be dispersed. Do not use oil-based gels if you are expecting the vet to come and

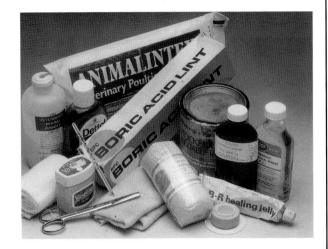

look at a wound, as they are not easy to remove.

Round-ended scissors - these are better than pointed end scissors for safety reasons. Use curved scissors to snip off hair around wounds.

Tweezers - must be used carefully if you are trying to extract a foreign body as you must be wary of causing further damage.

Cotton wool

Salt and antiseptic washes

Clean, large syringe - useful for flushing out a wound if a hose is not available.

How to take a horse's temperature

• Ensure the horse is held by a competent person.

• Make sure the thermometer is clean and sterile.

• Grease the bulb end with vaseline. Shake the thermometer down.

• Stand to the side of the horse's hindquarters to avoid being kicked.

• Use one hand to hold the horse's tail to one side. Insert the thermometer into the horse's rectum, using a gentle rotating movement.

• Hold the thermometer in position for one minute.

• Remove the thermometer and read it. Clean the thermometer before replacing it in your vet kit.

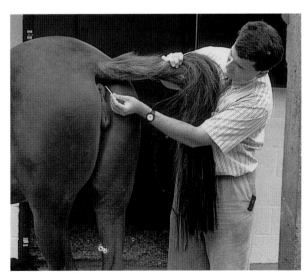

old foals (and it is vital that the pregnant mare is also wormed regularly). Failure to worm youngsters can have serious repercussions later in life - one charity rescue case I saw needed surgery, but worm damage to its major organs early in its life meant that it was highly unlikely to survive being under anaesthestic.

The difficulty with worms is that the damage they do is unseen. Horses suffer from a wide range of parasites, some of which live in the bowel, some in the lungs; the life cycle of each species is different.

The signs of an animal suffering from a worm burden are:

- weight loss
- staring coat
- tail rubbing
- coughing
- colic (stomach pain)
- diarrhoea
- anaemia
- jaundice

The signs vary according to the parasite involved and the level of infection.

Types of worms

Redworms or strongyles There are two types - large and small redworm - each affecting different areas of the horse. Both species are picked up by the horse grazing: the small redworm develop in and around the gut (forming cysts in the walls of the caecum and colon) while the large ones, which are the most devastasting of the species to affect equines, burrow through tissues, damaging blood vessels and organs.

The life-cycle of the large redworm is a long one - six to seven months from the ingestion by the horse to worm eggs eventually being expelled in dung and the cycle continuing.

Roundworms or ascarids These may grow to about a foot in length and can be as thick as a pencil. The roundworm's life cycle is extremely quick - around two months - but the eggs, when expelled on to the pasture, are extremely resilient and can lay on pasture, or indeed stable yards, for several years.

Pinworms or oxyuris A horse suffering with pinworm eggs under his tail will rub his tail due to the itchiness. These worms are usually pure white and may grow up to four inches in length. Their life cycle

takes around five months to complete.

Lungworms or dictyocaulus These are closely related to small redworms, but, as their name suggests, they end up in the lungs where the adult worms lay eggs. The horse coughs up and then swallows these eggs so they continue with their lifecycle in the same way that small redworms do, ie eventually being passed out with dung.

Tapeworms The worms mentioned so far are all true worms, but the tapeworm does not fit into this category. Tapeworms are made up of segments, each of which contains many eggs. When the tapeworm in the gut sheds a segment this is passed out on to the pasture where the segment decays and the eggs spread on to the land. These eggs are then eaten by tiny forage mites, which are in turn ingested by the horse. Within eight weeks the tapeworm matures and the cycle starts again.

Bots Although these are not worms, they are always considered as part of the horse's parasite control programme. Bots are the maggots of a fly which lays its eggs on the hair of horses in summer - they are easily spotted as they are whitish-yellow specks on the coat which are difficult to remove.

As the horse licks its coat or grooms another horse so the eggs are ingested. They hatch into maggots, burrowing through the horse's tissues until they reach the stomach where they stay throughout winter, eventually beign expelled with dung in spring.

It is essential that a control programme is operated, but this must cater for the different worms which are attacking the horses. Modern wormers are effective, but not all wormers can deal with all worms, and as some are more concentrated than others, you may need to use certain ones more often in order to achieve the same effect. Some worms have also built up resistance to a particular group of wormers (which is why it is recommended that you change wormers annually). It is therefore sensible to keep up to date with news on this front and also other veterinary research matters. (*Your Horse* magazine, for example, has a monthly article dealing with such news).

How to worm

Wormers are generally available as pastes in syringes or as granules in sachets. The granules can be mixed

Above right Adjusting a worming syringe so that the correct amount of paste for the animal's bodyweight is adminstered.

Right Adminstering a wormer orally.

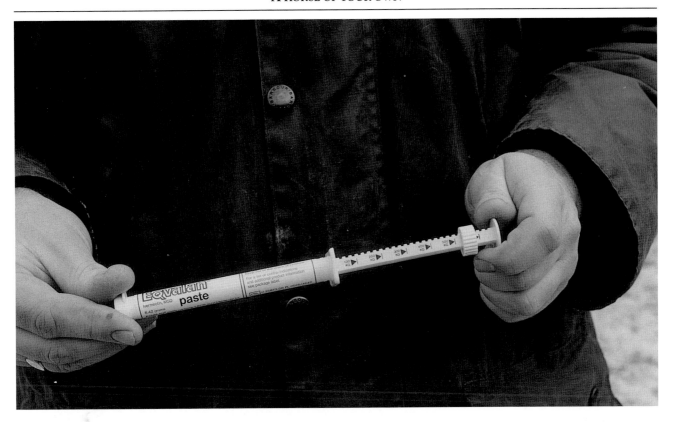

in with feed (use carrots, apples, etc, to tempt the horse is he is a fussy feeder). The syringe is inserted into the horse's mouth, in the gap between the incisors and molar teeth, and the plunger is depressed so the paste is spread on the horse's tongue.

When to worm

For horses spending time at pasture it is wise to worm every four weeks through summer and every six weeks through winter. If the wormer you use contains ivermectin (marketed as Eqvalan) this worming routine can be extended to every eight weeks throughout the year as this product is more concentrated and is the most effective general wormer.

You should use a double dose of Stongid P in midsummer as this is the only one which will shift tapeworms. The manufacturers also recommend that in the light of recent research upon tapeworms, that the double dose of Strongid P should be repeated in October. The only wormer which has an effect upon bots in Eqvalan, and this should be adminstered in winter.

Points to note:

• Always worm a new horse and keep the animal stabled for 48 hours afterwards, before he goes out on new pasture.

• Try to worm all the horses using the same grazing at the same time.

• You must know the horse's bodyweight in order to give him the correct dosage of wormer. It is better to slightly over-dose than not to give enough.

• If you think your horse has a worm problem your vet can arrange for a worm count to be done and acted upon.

• Pick up droppings every day from small pastures and at least twice a week from larger areas to avoid the pasture becoming over-infected with worms.

• If possible, rest your pasture for at least part of the year.

• Let other animals such as cattle and sheep graze with your horses as they help reduce the worm burden.

If you have got as far as this and not been deterred, if your horse is safely delivered and installed and insured, then I have not been able to persuade you to go the sensible route and buy a hamster. As a horse owner for the last 30 or so years, I am well aware of the joys and heartaches in store for you, and I wish you the very best of luck!

INDEX